GET SMART

Books by Kevin Johnson

Early Teen Devotionals

Can I Be a Christian Without Being Weird?
Could Someone Wake Me Up Before I Drool on the Desk?
Does Anybody Know What Planet My Parents Are From?
So Who Says I Have to Act My Age?
Was That a Balloon or Did Your Head Just Pop?
Who Should I Listen To?
Why Can't My Life Be a Summer Vacation?
Why Is God Looking for Friends?

Early Teen Discipleship

Get God: Make Friends With the King of the Universe
Wise Up: Stand Clear of the Unsmartness of Sin
Cross Train: Blast Through the Bible From Front to Back
Pray Hard: Talk to God With Total Confidence
See Jesus: Peer Into the Life and Mind of Your Master
Stick Tight: Glue Yourself to Godly Friends
Get Smart: Unscramble Mind-Boggling Questions of Your Faith
Bust Loose: Become the Wild New Person You Are in Jesus

Books for Youth

Catch the Wave!
Find Your Fit[1]
God's Will, God's Best[2]
Jesus Among Other Gods: Youth Edition[3]
Look Who's Toast Now!
What's With the Dudes at the Door?[4]
What's With the Mutant in the Microscope?[4]
What Do Ya Know?
Where Ya Gonna Go?

---

*To find out more about Kevin Johnson's books or speaking availability,
visit his Web site: www.thewave.org*

[1]with Jane Kise [2]with Josh McDowell [3]with Ravi Zacharias [4]with James White

● Unscramble Mind-Boggling Questions of Your Faith

GET SMART

Kevin Johnson

BETHANY HOUSE

MINNEAPOLIS, MINNESOTA

Published by Bethany House Publishers
A Ministry of Bethany Fellowship International
11400 Hampshire Avenue South
Bloomington, Minnesota 55438
www.bethanyhouse.com

Printed in the United States of America by
Bethany Press International, Bloomington, Minnesota 55438

Library of Congress Cataloging-in-Publication Data

Johnson, Kevin (Kevin Walter)
    Get smart : unscramble mind-boggling questions of your faith / by Kevin
Johnson.
        v. cm. — (Early teen discipleship)
    ISBN 0-7642-2435-2 (pbk.)
    1. Teenagers—Religious life—Miscellanea.   2. Christian life—Miscellanea.
[1. Christian life.]   I. Title.
    BV4531.3 .J645   2002
    248.8'3—dc21   2002002810

To youth everywhere

who get smart . . . get close to Jesus . . .

and let their knowledge of him

change their lives.

KEVIN JOHNSON is the bestselling author or co-author of more than twenty books for youth, including *Can I Be a Christian Without Being Weird?* and *Catch the Wave!* A full-time author and speaker, he served as senior editor for adult nonfiction at Bethany House Publishers and pastored a group of more than four hundred sixth through ninth graders at Elmbrook Church in metro Milwaukee. While his training includes an M.Div. from Fuller Theological Seminary and a B.A. in English and Print Journalism from the University of Wisconsin–River Falls, his current interests include cycling, swimming, and running. Kevin and his wife, Lyn, live in Minnesota with their three children—Nate, Karin, and Elise.

Contents

Part 3: Scrubbing Up Sin

Part 4: Grabbing God's Best

Part 5: Untangling Heaven and Hell

How to Use This Book

Welcome to *Get Smart*. This book is part of the EARLY TEEN DISCI-PLESHIP series, better remembered by its clever initials, ETD. I wrote ETD as a follow-up to my series of bestselling devotion-als—books like *Can I Be a Christian Without Being Weird?* and *Could Someone Wake Me Up Before I Drool on the Desk?* ETD has one aim: to help you take your next step in becoming wildly devoted to Jesus. If you're ready to work on a vital, heart-to-heart, sold-out relationship with God, this is your series.

The goal of *Get Smart* is to help you unscramble the mind-boggling questions of your faith. *Get Smart* prods you toward that goal through twenty-five Bible studies designed to make you think—okay, without *totally* breaking your brain. It will help you

- dig into Scripture on your own;
- feed on insights that you might not otherwise find;
- hit the heart issues that push you away from God or pull you closer to him.

You can pick your own pace—anything from a study a day to a study a week. But here's what you'll find in each study:

- Your first stop is BRAIN DRAIN—your spot at the beginning of each lesson to spout what you think.
- Then there's FLASHBACK—a bit of background so you better understand what's coming up.
- Don't skip over the BIBLE CHUNK—a hand-picked Bible pas-sage to read.
- You get STUFF TO KNOW—questions to help you dig into what a passage means.
- There's INSIGHT—facts about the passage you might not fig-ure out on your own.
- DA'SCOOP—definitions of weird words.
- And SIDELIGHT—other Bible verses that let you see the topic from a different angle.

The other big questions are, well . . .

- BIG QUESTIONS—your chance to apply what you have learned to your life.
- Each study wraps up with a DEEP THOT—a thought to chew on.

But that's not the end.

- There's STICKY STUFF—a Bible verse to jam into your brain juice.
- ACT ON IT—a way to do something with what you just learned.
- And DIG ON—another Bible passage to unearth if you want more.

And one more thing: There are cards in the back of the book for all the verses in STICKY STUFF, with a few bonus cards thrown in—since we'd already killed the tree.

If you've got a pencil and know how to use it, you're all set.

EXCEPT FOR ONE THING   You can study

Get Smart on your own. But you can also work through this book with a friend or in a group. After every five studies there's a page called "Talk About It." Nope—you don't have to cover every question on the page. There are too many to answer, so pick the ones that matter most to you.

Whenever you do an ETD study with one friend or a bunch, keep in mind three goals—and three big questions to help you remember those goals. And nope—you don't have to actually ask those questions each time, because that would feel canned. But each time you meet you want to

- EMPATHIZE: *What's gone on since the last time you got together?* To "empathize" means to put yourself in someone else's shoes. Galatians 6:2 tells us to "carry each other's burdens" (NIV), or to "share each other's troubles and problems" (NLT). Whether you call them "highs and lows," "wows and pows," "uppers and downers," or "wins and wedgies," take time to celebrate and support each other by chatting through life's important happenings and offering simple, to-the-point prayers.
- ENCOURAGE: *Where are you at with Jesus?* Hebrews 3:13 says to

"encourage one another daily. . . so that none of you may be hardened by sin's deceitfulness." Religious rules apart from a relationship with God are deadly. So instead be real: Are you growing closer to or wandering away from the Lord you're learning to follow? Is anything tripping you up?

- EQUIP: *What one truth are you going to take away from today that will help you live closer to Jesus?* Second Timothy 3:16–17 promises that "All Scripture is inspired by God and is useful to teach us what is true and to make us realize what is wrong in our lives. It straightens us out and teaches us to do what is right. It is God's way of preparing us in every way, fully equipped for every good thing God wants us to do" (NLT). Don't leave your get-together without one point of truth that will make a difference in your life. It might not be the thought or verse that anyone else picks. But grab at least one truth—and hang on tight by letting it make a difference in your life.

Got it? Not only is *Get Smart* a study to do on your own, but better yet, it can help you grow your faith with your friends. You can pick a leader—a youth or adult—or take turns picking questions and talking through them as your time allows. Just keep the three big goals in mind.

Now you're ready. You can do it. Grow ahead and turn the page and get started.

PART 1

DIGGING FOR GOD

1. Super Defender of the Faith

Where am I going to get answers about God?

You would have survived okay when your friends started pelting you with really tough spiritual questions—if only you'd been able to find a phone booth. But with nowhere to change into your superhero-defender-of-the-faith long undies, you just didn't have the answers you needed. Their questions reduced you to a quivering mass of "Well, um, *huff*, I don't know . . . *sigh*."

BRAIN DRAIN How do you expect to get a hold of life-altering answers about God?

FLASHBACK You probably have some friends who feel close to God sitting on a mountaintop or wandering through cool forests. That idea makes some Christians squirm. But before you jump on those friends, realize that they're half right. They *can* look around the world and learn some facts about God—and *it says so right in your Bible*. But beware: If you only know God from what you see in the world, your knowledge will be *limited*. And because all people are sinful, your view of him will be *flawed*. If you want the whole truth and nothing but the truth about God, there's another place you need to look.

BIBLE CHUNK Read Psalm 19:1–10

(1) The heavens declare the glory of God;
the skies proclaim the work of his hands.

(2) Day after day they pour forth speech;
   night after night they display knowledge.
(3) There is no speech or language
   where their voice is not heard.
(4) Their voice goes out into all the earth,
   their words to the ends of the world.
   In the heavens he has pitched a tent for the sun,
(5) which is like a bridegroom coming forth from his pavilion,
   like a champion rejoicing to run his course.
(6) It rises at one end of the heavens
   and makes its circuit to the other;
   nothing is hidden from its heat.
(7) The law of the Lord is perfect,
   reviving the soul.
   The statutes of the Lord are trustworthy,
   making wise the simple.
(8) The precepts of the Lord are right,
   giving joy to the heart.
   The commands of the Lord are radiant,
   giving light to the eyes.
(9) The fear of the Lord is pure,
   enduring forever.
   The ordinances of the Lord are sure
   and altogether righteous.
(10) They are more precious than gold,
   than much pure gold;
   they are sweeter than honey,
   than honey from the comb.

STUFF TO KNOW What exactly do you know about God by glancing around the world? Hint: Who is saying what about whom (verse 1)?

DA'SCOOP The sky screams of God's *glory*. That's his awestriking majesty and splendor—his jaw-dropping perfection and power. Looking at the sun and stars and lots of other stuff tells you an all-mighty God created the world.

Exactly how far does this news spread? Is there anywhere on

earth that doesn't get the scoop about God (verses 3–4)?

SIDELIGHT There's no place you can go where God's glory doesn't shine. Get this: His handiwork is so unmistakable that all people know—deep down—that God exists. Romans 1:19–20 says, "For the truth about God is known to them instinctively. God has put this knowledge in their hearts. From the time the world was created, people have seen the earth and sky and all that God made. They can clearly see his invisible qualities—his eternal power and divine nature. So they have no excuse whatsoever for not knowing God" (NLT).

Okay. You can find out about God from his *works*. How else do you figure out who he is (verse 7)?

Spot it? You find out about God not just by his *works* but by his *words*. So answer this: How good are God's *laws, statutes, precepts, commands*, and *ordinances*? What do they do for you (verses 7–10)?

DA'SCOOP In Bible lingo *the law* covers everything God's Word reveals about him. It isn't just *do's* and *don'ts*.

BIG QUESTIONS Think hard: If you ignored the Bible, what would you lack in your knowledge of God?

INSIGHT Looking around your world tells you there's a God who created the universe. But people so badly twist what creation tells them about the creator that God's true identity gets lost (Romans 1:21–32). So if you want the unwarped truth about God, you need the Bible. It tells you everything you need to know about the God who made everything. It's where you find out about Jesus, God's hugest revelation of himself. And it informs you that "the Word [Jesus] became human and lived here on earth among us. He was full of unfailing love and faithfulness. And we have seen his glory, the glory of the only Son of the Father" (John 1:14 NLT).

How would you explain to a non-Christian friend how to find out who God really is?

DEEP THOT Creation gives you a knowledge of God you can't deny. But if you want to catch all of who God is—including how you can spend eternity with him in heaven—you've got to look at his book.

STICKY STUFF Psalm 19:1, 7 reminds you to grab hold of both God's *works* and his *words*. There's a card in the back to help you stuff that verse in your brain.

ACT ON IT Make a list of what you see about God's greatness through his creation. Make another list of what you know about God through his Word.

DIG ON Read that passage in Romans 1:21–32 to see how humankind buries its knowledge of God.

2. Facts, Feelings, Faces
Why believe the Bible?

With less than a half hour of study time free each day at school, Megan usually worked at a table in the library frantically getting done whatever she could. Today, though, she curled up in a cushy chair and pulled out a small Bible. She wasn't trying to be a religious freakazoid. After getting whipped by a surprise quiz in math, she needed to recharge. It was a relaxing moment— until her classmate Rita walked up, that is. "The Bible?" she smirked. "You read the Bible? That's stupid."

BRAIN DRAIN Why do you read the Bible? Why do you believe it—or not?

FLASHBACK Lots of people who mock the Bible have never bothered to find out why it's worth reading—or worth believing. In this Bible Chunk, the apostle Paul is near death, penning a letter to Timothy (2 Timothy 4:6–7). He knows Timothy will be a key person to carry on the Christian faith (2 Timothy 1:13–14) and that Timothy's own faith will be tested (2 Timothy 1:8–9). And Paul gives Timothy three reasons *why* the Bible's message will be worth giving his life to.

BIBLE CHUNK Read 2 Timothy 3:10–17

(10) You, however, know all about my teaching, my way of life, my purpose, faith, patience, love, endurance, (11) persecutions, sufferings—what kinds of things happened to me in Antioch, Iconium and Lystra, the

persecutions I endured. Yet the Lord rescued me from all of them. (12) In fact, everyone who wants to live a godly life in Christ Jesus will be persecuted, (13) while evil men and impostors will go from bad to worse, deceiving and being deceived. (14) But as for you, continue in what you have learned and have become convinced of, because you know those from whom you learned it, (15) and how from infancy you have known the holy Scriptures, which are able to make you wise for salvation through faith in Christ Jesus. (16) All Scripture is God-breathed and is useful for teaching, rebuking, correcting and training in righteousness, (17) so that the man of God may be thoroughly equipped for every good work.

STUFF TO KNOW Why do you suppose Paul reminds Timothy that Tim knows all about him (verses 13–15)?

Do you think Paul is a reliable source of info about God (verses 10–13)? How about those other people who taught Tim "from infancy" (verse 15)? Why or why not?

INSIGHT Reason #1 the Bible is believable: FACES. Paul dares to say that he and the people who trained Timothy in the faith—his mother and grandmother (2 Timothy 1:5)—are worth trusting. Like Timothy, you can size up the credibility of Paul, the other writers of Scripture, and the people in your own life who have taught you the Bible. Best yet, you can size up the trustworthiness of the God revealed in the Bible. Paul looked at God and called him "the one in whom I trust" (2 Timothy 1:12 NLT).

Who is the source of the Bible (verse 16)?

INSIGHT For lots of people, trusting the people who tell

you the Bible is true isn't enough. They want FACTS. Well, the Bible claims to be perfectly inspired by God—*God-breathed*. And there's a load of evidence that the Bible is a one-of-a-kind book that could only come from God:

- The Bible presents a *tight message* of God saving humankind—without contradicting itself—even though it contains *sixty-six books* written over *fifteen hundred years* by some *forty authors*.
- The actual *words* of the Bible are well established. The number, age, and quality of Bible manuscripts far exceeds those of any other ancient document.
- The *events* in the Bible took place in real times and real places—facts verified by archaeology.
- Hundreds of Bible *prophecies* came true in Christ. And those predictions were spoken hundreds of years before his birth. Who but an all-knowing God could write that kind of book?
- The Bible's truthfulness is backed up by the astounding fact of *Christ's rising from the dead*—more on that in Study 9.

So what's the Bible supposed to *do* for Timothy—and anyone else who follows its teachings (verses 15–16)?

SIDELIGHT When you test the Bible's teachings in real life you find that they *work*. The point? Not only do FACTS and FACES convince you the Bible is true, but in time your FEELINGS will too. Jesus, in fact, suggests this test: "If anyone chooses to do God's will, he will find out whether my teaching comes from God or whether I speak on my own" (John 7:17).

BIG QUESTIONS Who are the FACES who make the Bible believable for you?

How have you been struck by FEELINGS that the Bible rings true—that it works in real life?

What FACTS about the Bible do you find most persuasive?

DEEP THOT The Bible's truth is absolute—true in all times and places, whether you believe it or not. But the Bible itself gives you reasons to believe its message. Think hard about the FACTS. Size up the FACES. And if you test out the Bible in real life, sooner or later you'll get smacked by deep FEELINGS of its truth.

STICKY STUFF Second Timothy 3:16 is one of the tastiest chunks in the Bible. Chew on it.

ACT ON IT You could spend the rest of your life studying the great reasons to believe the Bible. If you doubt the Bible's believability, check out the section on "Myths About the Bible" in the ultrapopular book *Don't Check Your Brains at the Door* by Josh McDowell and Bob Hostetler.

DIG ON Second Peter 1:21 gives you a glimpse into how the content of the Bible came to be.

(3.) Primordial Ooze
Where did the world come from?

Time-warped back to the beginning of earth's history, you stand barefoot in a two-inch-deep puddle of ooze. Behold! In that insignificant puddle dwells earth's first life-form—the way-back ancestor of one of those single-cell amoebas you study in science class. Careful! You've got the future of your planet swimming between your toes. Wiggle the wrong way and life will never arise on planet earth . . . and you will cease to exist.

BRAIN DRAIN Where do you think the world came from? Could you go back to a puddle of ooze and squeeze out life?

FLASHBACK If you want to make any sense of the Bible, you need to wrestle with its first ten words: "In the beginning God created the heavens and the earth." But those ultra-important words might not match up to what your science book at school says. This chunk is the longest in *Get Smart*—but it's worth a big look at what the Bible says about the origin of your world.

BIBLE CHUNK Read Genesis 1:1–25

(1) In the beginning God created the heavens and the earth. (2) Now the earth was formless and empty, darkness was over the surface of the deep, and the Spirit of God was hovering over the waters.

(3) And God said, "Let there be light," and there was light. (4) God saw that the light was good, and he separated the light from the darkness. (5) God called the light "day" and the darkness he called "night." And there was evening, and there was morning—the first day.

(6) And God said, "Let there be an expanse between the waters to separate water from water." (7) So God made the expanse and separated the water under the expanse from the water above it. And it was so. (8) God called the expanse "sky." And there was evening, and there was morning—the second day.

(9) And God said, "Let the water under the sky be gathered to one place, and let dry ground appear." And it was so. (10) God called the dry ground "land," and the gathered waters he called "seas." And God saw that it was good.

(11) Then God said, "Let the land produce vegetation: seed-bearing plants and trees on the land that bear fruit with seed in it, according to their various kinds." And it was so. (12) The land produced vegetation: plants bearing seed according to their kinds and trees bearing fruit with seed in it according to their kinds. And God saw that it was good. (13) And there was evening, and there was morning—the third day.

(14) And God said, "Let there be lights in the expanse of the sky to separate the day from the night, and let them serve as signs to mark seasons and days and years, (15) and let them be lights in the expanse of the sky to give light on the earth." And it was so. (16) God made two great lights—the greater light to govern the day and the lesser light to govern the night. He also made the stars. (17) God set them in the expanse of the sky to give light on the earth, (18) to govern the day and the night, and to separate light from darkness. And God saw that it was good. (19) And there was evening, and there was morning—the fourth day.

(20) And God said, "Let the water teem with living creatures, and let birds fly above the earth across the expanse of the sky." (21) So God created the great creatures of the sea and every living and moving thing with which the water teems, according to their kinds, and every winged bird according to its kind. And God saw that it was good. (22) God blessed them and said, "Be fruitful and increase in number and fill the water in the seas, and let the birds increase on the earth." (23) And there was evening, and there was morning—the fifth day.

(24) And God said, "Let the land produce living creatures according to their kinds: livestock, creatures that move along the ground, and wild animals, each according to its kind." And it was so. (25) God made the wild animals according to their kinds, the livestock according to their kinds, and all the creatures that move along the ground according to their kinds. And God saw that it was good.

STUFF TO KNOW What was the world like before God "created the heavens and the earth" (verses 1–2)?

DA'SCOOP Big point: "Formless and void" means there was nothing there. God started from scratch.

What all did God make? Jot some notes—or circle the God-made stuff back in the Bible Chunk (verses 1–25).

BIG QUESTIONS How does what you learn from science match—or not—what you read in the Bible about creation?

What bugs you most about how the Bible explains the beginning of the world? Why is it the way it is?

True or false: The Bible's explanation was meant for stupid people who lived before science—and creation and evolution really say the same thing.

INSIGHT Even though the Bible was first written before the rise of modern science, you can't dismiss the Bible as a dumbed-down version of science. The Bible's concern is more *who* made the world and *what* he made than *how* he made it, and the Bible's biggest origin-of-the-world claim is that *God created everything.* Darwinian evolution says that everything in the world got here through *random natural forces*—that is, totally apart from any involvement by God. That's hardly the same thing.

Is it possible that the world came to be without any direction from God? Why or why not?

INSIGHT You wouldn't look at a computer and assume it was assembled by shaking parts in a box. A computer shows obvious signs of *design.* Well, nature is jammed with infinitely more complex marvels—like you, for example—that show an *intricacy* and *interdependence* that doesn't happen apart from the work of an *intelligent designer.*

DEEP THOT The biggest conflict between the theory of evolution and the Bible isn't the *process* but the *person*—that evolution leaves out God. Your world didn't come about by chance. It came into existence by the choice of God.

STICKY STUFF Grab hold of Genesis 1:1. It's a better explanation of you than ooze.

ACT ON IT Want to learn more about the Bible and the origin of life on planet earth? Grab a book I co-wrote with James White called *What's With the Mutant in the Microscope?*

DIG ON Read Hebrews 11:3 to see creation-out-of-nothing in the New Testament.

4. Rat Trash
Is God down on people?

Nicole was surprised the most popular boy in school wanted to sign her yearbook. But Matt didn't exactly seal his signature with a smooch and a phone number. "All year long I've been thinking . . ." he wrote, "that you're a waste of space. You're an air-hogging, melon-headed offspring of a moron. What I can't figure out is this: Why were you ever born?"

BRAIN DRAIN Hmmm . . . why do you think *you* exist? What good are you to the rest of the people on planet earth?

FLASHBACK Some peers—and other people—might say you're as valuable as trash rejected by a rat. Truth is, that's how lots of people think God sees people—like we're the scum of the solar system, the maggots of the universe, the phlegm of the—got the picture? They're wrong, of course. Look at what this psalm says.

BIBLE CHUNK Read Psalm 8:1–8

(1) O Lord, our Lord,
    how majestic is your name in all the earth!
    You have set your glory
    above the heavens.
(2) From the lips of children and infants
    you have ordained praise
    because of your enemies,

to silence the foe and the avenger.
(3) When I consider your heavens,
the work of your fingers,
the moon and the stars,
which you have set in place,
(4) what is man that you are mindful of him,
the son of man that you care for him?
(5) You made him a little lower than the heavenly beings
and crowned him with glory and honor.
(6) You made him ruler over the works of your hands;
you put everything under his feet:
(7) all flocks and herds,
and the beasts of the field,
(8) the birds of the air,
and the fish of the sea,
all that swim the paths of the seas.

STUFF TO KNOW Back up and review what you
learned in the first Bible Chunk in *Get Smart*. What does David
think of God? What has he been looking at to convince him of
that fact (verses 1, 3)?

God wants someone to say how great he is. Who? What will
their praise do (verse 2)?

SIDELIGHT You don't have to be simple, slow, or stupid
to worship God. You do need a child's humble awe of God's
greatness. Jesus, in fact, said that "unless you turn from your
sins and become as little children, you will never get into the
Kingdom of Heaven. Therefore, anyone who becomes as humble as this little child is the greatest in the Kingdom of Heaven"
(Matthew 18:3–4 NLT).

David ponders the magnificent universe God has made. And he
thinks something shrinks to insignificance in comparison. What

is it (verse 4)? What exactly is David saying?

Human beings seem more than a tad insignificant in the universe. To some people they might seem like trash. But what's our real status in the universe (verse 5)?

SIDELIGHT The Hebrew words for "a little lower than the heavenly beings" could mean either "a little lower than the angels" or even "a little lower than God." Either way, you're awestriking stuff, made in God's image (Genesis 1:26–27).

What responsibilities does God give people to prove he's given them great gifts (verses 6–8)?

BIG QUESTIONS So God thinks people have mind-boggling worth. But he just feels that way about Christians, right? Explain how you know.

SIDELIGHT God has some gut-wrenchingly nasty things to say about people—like the truth that all people are sinful. But that factoid—that all people have rebelled against him—also includes Christians (Romans 3:23). And this factoid—that God has given all people great worth—includes people who don't know Jesus.

How are you supposed to look at yourself—now that you know God made you so great?

SIDELIGHT God isn't looking for groveling. He's looking for gratitude. Everything you have—and are—are gifts from God. Like Paul asked the people in Corinth: What do you have that you didn't get from God (1 Corinthians 4:7)?

How can you react next time you're slammed and led to believe you're worthless? Or the next time you want to trash-talk someone?

DEEP THOT God hasn't crowned you King of Creation. That's his title alone. But he gives you and all the other occupants of your planet an unbelievable portion of his glory. He made you way more than rat trash.

STICKY STUFF Psalm 8:5–6 will remind you that God made people great.

ACT ON IT Make a list of people you've thought are somehow subhuman. And do something that shows respect for each one.

DIG ON Look at Psalm 139:13–16, which says God made people awesome.

5. Who Owns You?
Who owns the universe?

Picture the biggest crowd you've ever seen—maybe fifty or sixty thousand spectators jammed into a stadium. Or mobs you've seen on TV—like millions packing the National Mall in Washington, D.C. Now ponder this: How many of those people know that every breath they take—and every move they make— belongs to God? Not many. But whether they want to or not, every person will someday acknowledge that Jesus Christ is King of the Universe.

BRAIN DRAIN What does it matter that God made the world?

FLASHBACK God has shown himself to the human race—in creation, in the Bible, and in Jesus. He made you great. Now here's where God gets personal. Truth is, there's no escaping God's ownership of the universe. And there's no dodging God's plan for you. And you wouldn't want to.

BIBLE CHUNK Read Psalm 50:1–23

(1) The Mighty One, God, the Lord,
   speaks and summons the earth
   from the rising of the sun to the place where it sets.
(2) From Zion, perfect in beauty,
   God shines forth.
(3) Our God comes and will not be silent;
   a fire devours before him,

and around him a tempest rages.
(4) He summons the heavens above,
and the earth, that he may judge his people:
(5) "Gather to me my consecrated ones,
who made a covenant with me by sacrifice."
(6) And the heavens proclaim his righteousness,
for God himself is judge.
Selah
(7) "Hear, O my people, and I will speak,
O Israel, and I will testify against you:
I am God, your God.
(8) I do not rebuke you for your sacrifices
or your burnt offerings, which are ever before me.
(9) I have no need of a bull from your stall
or of goats from your pens,
(10) for every animal of the forest is mine,
and the cattle on a thousand hills.
(11) I know every bird in the mountains,
and the creatures of the field are mine.
(12) If I were hungry I would not tell you,
for the world is mine, and all that is in it.
(13) Do I eat the flesh of bulls
or drink the blood of goats?
(14) Sacrifice thank offerings to God,
fulfill your vows to the Most High,
(15) and call upon me in the day of trouble;
I will deliver you, and you will honor me."
(16) But to the wicked, God says:
"What right have you to recite my laws
or take my covenant on your lips?
(17) You hate my instruction
and cast my words behind you.
(18) When you see a thief, you join with him;
you throw in your lot with adulterers.
(19) You use your mouth for evil
and harness your tongue to deceit.
(20) You speak continually against your brother
and slander your own mother's son.
(21) These things you have done and I kept silent;
you thought I was altogether like you.
But I will rebuke you
and accuse you to your face.
(22) "Consider this, you who forget God,
or I will tear you to pieces, with none to rescue:

S(23) He who sacrifices thank offerings honors me,
and he prepares the way
so that I may show him the salvation of God."

STUFF TO KNOW There's a whole wad of ideas

jammed into those first few verses. Here's one big one: What all
is God in charge of (verses 1–5)?

The folks in verses 7–8 are trying to wow God with their gung-
ho religion. Does God need anything they can give him (verses
9–13)?

Get it straight: What all does God oversee as King of the Universe? Does he leave anything out (verses 9–12)?

What does God actually want from us (verses 14–15)?

INSIGHT Got it? God gives you three basic jobs: Say

thanks when he helps you, keep your promise to follow him,
and call on him when you get in trouble.

What's wrong with the wicked? What are they up to (verses 16–
20)?

Does God smoke evildoers right away (verse 21)?

BIG QUESTIONS What gives God the right to run the universe?

INSIGHT It's simple: You make it, you own it—whether it's a clay pot or the whole creation.

How excited are you about submitting your whole life to the God who made you?

DEEP THOT Flash forward: Philippians 2:9–10 says that at the end of time every knee will bow and every mouth admit that Jesus Christ is Lord. And here's why: God made you. He owns you. But as you'll find out next, he's totally worth giving your life to.

STICKY STUFF Keep it simple: Psalm 50:12.

ACT ON IT Make a list of all the things in your life you think you own—your time, your talents, your treasures. Then pray through your list and tell God that everything about you belongs to him.

DIG ON Isaiah 43:1–13 says more about your King.

Talk About It • 1

EMPATHIZE: What's going on in your life?
ENCOURAGE: How are you doing with Jesus?
EQUIP: What one truth will you take home today?

- What exactly do you know about God by glancing around the world? How far does this news spread? (Study 1)
- If you ignored the Bible, what would you lack in your knowledge of God? (Study 1)
- How would you explain to a non-Christian friend how to find out who God really is? (Study 1)
- Why do you read the Bible? Why do you believe it—or not? (Study 2)
- How does the Bible persuade us through its FACTS, FEELINGS, and FACES? (Study 2)
- True or false: The Bible's explanation was meant for stupid people who lived before science—and creation and evolution really say the same thing. (Study 3)
- Is it possible that the world came to be without any direction from God? Why or why not? (Study 3)
- Why do you think *you* exist? What good are you to the rest of the people on planet earth? (Study 4)
- What does God say about your place in the universe? (Study 4)
- What difference does it make to your everyday life that God made the world? (Study 5)
- How excited are you about submitting your whole life to the God who made you? (Study 5)

PART 2

SPOTTING YOUR SAVIOR

6. God in a Bod
Who was Jesus?

Okay, so you've never actually seen the God who formed the world from nothing—or who stretched out the heavens. So besides looking at creation, what else can buff up your belief in God? After all, most people want an unmistakably clear sign that God *exists*—and obvious evidence of *who he is*. The only thing that will satisfy them is spotting God up close and personal. And that's exactly why Jesus came to planet earth.

BRAIN DRAIN So what makes you think Jesus was more than just another nicey-nice religious guy?

FLASHBACK This Bible Chunk calls Jesus "the Word," a very clever expression. To the people who first read this passage, it meant that (1) Jesus communicates God's message; (2) Jesus possesses God's one-of-a-kind power to create stuff; (3) Jesus is the bright mind that runs the universe; and (4) Jesus is God himself. Those are huge claims. Have a look for yourself. . . .

BIBLE CHUNK Read John 1:1–5, 10–14

(1) In the beginning was the Word, and the Word was with God, and the Word was God. (2) He was with God in the beginning.

(3) Through him all things were made; without him nothing was made that has been made. (4) In him was life, and that life was the light of men. (5) The light shines in the darkness, but the darkness has not understood it.

(10) He was in the world, and though the world was made through him, the world did not recognize him. (11) He came to that which was his own, but his own did not receive him. (12) Yet to all who received him, to those who believed in his name, he gave the right to become children of God—(13) children born not of natural descent, nor of human decision or a husband's will, but born of God.

(14) The Word became flesh and lived for a while among us. We have seen his glory, the glory of the one and only Son, who came from the Father, full of grace and truth.

STUFF TO KNOW Everybody who got this Bible book would have known that Jesus was an extraordinary man who strolled through Israel. But this chunk says Jesus was way more than they could imagine. How long has Jesus been hanging around (verses 1–2)?

SIDELIGHT Heard those opening words before? "In the beginning" is the first phrase of the first book of the Bible. The words don't refer to a time in history but to a timeless eternity. Whatever Jesus is, he's been forever.

Jesus was three things. What (verse 1)? In the beginning . . .

• the Word _____

• the Word was _____

• and the Word was _____

INSIGHT Those three statements leave no doubt about three facts: (1) Jesus has existed forever; (2) he is equal and separate from God; (3) yet he is also God himself. The Bible presents Jesus as *God's Son*. This chunk also shows him as *God in a body*.

So what else did Jesus do (verse 3)?

SIDELIGHT Surprised? Together with the Holy Spirit, God the Father and God the Son form a union so tight it can only be called a *trinity*—a "tri-unity." That's tough stuff to grasp, but it's a teaching that runs from the front to the back of the Bible. As one member of that trinity, Jesus was indispensable to creation. Colossians 1:16 says, "For by him all things were created: things in heaven and on earth, visible and invisible."

How do some folks react to Jesus (verses 5, 10–11)?

How do others react? And what happens to them (verse 12)?

INSIGHT "Receiving Jesus" means believing *who he is* and *what he has done for you.* It's how you become part of God's family forever.

Sum it up: What can you see in Jesus (verse 14)?

BIG QUESTIONS Verse 14 packs a wallop: Jesus shows off God's *glory*—the bright shiny power of God. So what do *you* see when you look at Jesus?

If a friend wants to know about God, where are you going to tell him or her to look? Why?

DEEP THOT If you wonder what God is like, you've spotted the answer in Jesus. The Bible relays the astounding fact that in Jesus, God became a human being and lived among us. Hebrews 1:3 says that "The Son is the radiance of God's glory and the exact representation of his being, sustaining all things by his powerful word." Better than any sign in the sky, Jesus is God's ultimate Word. He shows you exactly who God is.

STICKY STUFF John 1:14 tells you that when you see Jesus, you've spotted God in a bod.

ACT ON IT Jesus did a ton of stuff (John 21:25). If you want to read about the mind and mission of your Master, check out the EARLY TEEN DISCIPLESHIP book *See Jesus*.

DIG ON Check out some of the Bible's other supreme statements about Jesus in Colossians 1:15–20 and Hebrews 1:1–14.

(7.) God So Loved
How can I have a relationship with God?

An old church stood proudly in the middle of a nameless small town, its steeple piercing the sky. As the town had decayed, so had the church. Hardly anyone attended anymore, but Rachel had heard there was a new young pastor in town. One evening she snuck into a dim back corner of the sanctuary and sat in a pew, looking up at the stained glass and wondering where God was. When the pastor spotted her as he locked up the building, they got to talking. "My parents never say anything about God— except to swear," Rachel told him. "I think I need God. But I don't know where to start."

BRAIN DRAIN Where would you start your search if you wanted to get to know God?

FLASHBACK One night way back in Bible times a religious leader named Nicodemus snuck through the dark to visit Jesus. Nicodemus is smart enough to see that only God's power can explain the miracles Jesus had done. But Jesus tells Nicodemus that a real relationship with God only starts when a person is spiritually reborn. While Nicodemus puzzles over that one, Jesus explains how *he* is the way to that fresh relationship with God. This Bible Chunk includes the Bible's most famous words—John 3:16. It also includes the words that follow—the rest of the message you might never have read before.

BIBLE CHUNK Read John 3:16–21

(16) "For God so loved the world that he gave his one and only Son, that whoever believes in him shall not perish but have eternal life. (17) For God did not send his Son into the world to condemn the world, but to save the world through him. (18) Whoever believes in him is not condemned, but whoever does not believe stands condemned already because he has not believed in the name of God's one and only Son. (19) This is the verdict: Light has come into the world, but men loved darkness instead of light because their deeds were evil. (20) Everyone who does evil hates the light, and will not come into the light for fear that his deeds will be exposed. (21) But whoever lives by the truth comes into the light, so that it may be seen plainly that what he has done has been done through God."

STUFF TO KNOW So what all did God give? Why (verse 16)?

If you believe Jesus is who he claims to be, what gift does God give you (verse 16)?

Does it sound like God sent Jesus to spy on human beings and remind you how rotten you are? What did Jesus really come to do (verse 17)?

So you believe in Jesus. Explain it again: What good does that do you (verse 18)?

Suppose you *don't* believe in Jesus. What's the consequence (verse 18)?

Some people don't accept Jesus. How come (verse 19)?

INSIGHT There's no difference in the *guilt* of Christians and non-Christians. All people have done evil, sinning against God and others (Romans 3:23). The difference between Christians and non-Christians is their *response* to God. Unbelievers hide from God. Believers get close to him so they can be healed. They not only admit they've done wrong, but they accept that God sent his Son as the sacrifice for the sins.

SIDELIGHT Colossians 1:13–14 tells exactly what happens when you believe—how God plucks you out of darkness and deposits you in a much better place: "For he has rescued us from the one who rules in the kingdom of darkness, and he has brought us into the Kingdom of his dear Son. God has purchased our freedom with his blood and has forgiven all our sins" (NLT).

BIG QUESTIONS Get personal: Do you believe in Jesus the way this Bible Chunk talks about?

So you're supposed to believe. What kind of belief do you think is "good enough" for God?

SIDELIGHT Just having any old belief isn't the stuff that saves you. Believing is humbly trusting that Christ died and rose for you. Ephesians 2:8–9 explains that nothing you can do is good enough to make God your friend: "God saved you by his special favor when you believed. And you can't take credit for this; it is a gift from God. Salvation is not a reward for the good things we have done, so none of us can boast about it" (NLT). "Grace" is God's unearned favor—and it means getting to know God is a total gift!

This Bible Chunk promises that God saves people who believe in Jesus—and that he gives them the gift of eternal life with him in heaven. How would you explain that to a friend?

DEEP THOT Believing in God isn't just jamming facts in your head. It's putting your trust in all of who Jesus is—who he is, what he teaches, and what he accomplished for you through his death on the cross.

STICKY STUFF Stick John 3:16 in your cerebrum. Stick in John 3:17 as well.

ACT ON IT Have you ever acted in a condemning way toward someone who doesn't yet trust in Jesus? Anything you can do about that now?

DIG ON Have a look at that whole chunk in Ephesians 2:1–10.

8. One Way?
Is Jesus the only way to get to heaven?

Anita signed up for a south-of-the-border mission trip expecting salsa, souvenirs, and stuffed shopping bags. She brought back Jesus instead. When she told her favorite aunt that she'd just discovered what it was like to have a close relationship with God, she hardly got the enthusiasm she expected. "I'm glad you feel closer to God, Anita," her aunt goozed. "Christianity is great for you—but there are lots of ways to know God. I feel like I have what I need. Can you understand that?"

BRAIN DRAIN Does God really expect everyone to become a Christian—or are other spiritual beliefs just as good? Explain.

FLASHBACK The Bible is blunt. Acts 4:12, for example, says that "There is salvation in no one else! There is no other name in all of heaven for people to call on to save them" (NLT). Some people who don't like that idea loudly disagree. Others just try to twist the Bible itself to say something else. Even if you've been taught that "Jesus is the only way to heaven," you need to digest for yourself what Jesus says in this Bible Chunk—because sooner or later someone will try to talk you out of your belief.

BIBLE CHUNK Read John 14:1–11

(1) "Do not let your hearts be troubled. Trust in God; trust also in me.
(2) In my Father's house are many rooms; if it were not so, I would have

told you. I am going there to prepare a place for you. (3) And if I go and prepare a place for you, I will come back and take you to be with me that you also may be where I am. (4) You know the way to the place where I am going."

(5) Thomas said to him, "Lord, we don't know where you are going, so how can we know the way?"

(6) Jesus answered, "I am the way and the truth and the life. No one comes to the Father except through me. (7) If you really knew me, you would know my Father as well. From now on, you do know him and have seen him."

(8) Philip said, "Lord, show us the Father and that will be enough for us."

(9) Jesus answered: "Don't you know me, Philip, even after I have been among you such a long time? Anyone who has seen me has seen the Father. How can you say, 'Show us the Father'? (10) Don't you believe that I am in the Father, and that the Father is in me? The words I say to you are not just my own. Rather, it is the Father, living in me, who is doing his work. (11) Believe me when I say that I am in the Father and the Father is in me; or at least believe on the evidence of the miracles themselves.

STUFF TO KNOW Where is Jesus headed (verses 1–3)?

How come? What's Jesus going to do there (verses 2–3)?

INSIGHT Jesus doesn't fill in the details here on what heaven will be like. But like the late Christian musician Keith Green once said, "I look around at the world, and I see all the beauty that God made. I see the forests and the trees and all the things. And it says in the Bible that he made them in six days. . . . If this world took six days—and that home took two thousand years—this is living in a garbage can compared to what's going up there."

Jesus' disciple Thomas protests. What doesn't he know? Where does he want to go (verse 5)?

Jesus gives Thomas some directions—but not the kind Tom expected. How does Jesus say his disciples will get to that snazzy home he's preparing for his followers (verse 6)?

Look at the words that come straight from the mouth of Jesus. Does he think there's an alternate route to get to God's home in heaven (verse 6)?

Why is Jesus the only one who can offer accurate directions (verses 7–11)?

SIDELIGHT Jesus isn't just the only one who *knows* the way to the Father. He's the only one who *opened the way* for you to get there. The Bible says that the penalty for sin is death—not just physically dying, but being separated from God (Romans 6:23). And Jesus is the only person in history who paid the price for sin that God requires. First Timothy 2:5–6 explains, "There is only one God and one Mediator who can reconcile God and people. He is the man Christ Jesus. He gave his life to purchase freedom for everyone" (NLT).

BIG QUESTIONS Do you agree that Jesus is the one way to get to know God? Why or why not?

Suppose someone says that all religions work equally well in getting people acquainted with God—and scoring seats in heaven. How would you explain what makes Christianity unique—and uniquely effective?

DEEP THOT Lots of religious wise guys have been born, taught, and died. But the Bible teaches that Jesus was God become man. He taught. Even though he was sinless (Hebrews 4:15), he suffered death in our place. And to cap it off, he rose from the dead. He's a one-of-a-kind Savior who offers you a one-of-a-kind promise of eternal life with God.

STICKY STUFF John 14:6 tells you where you're headed—and how to get there.

ACT ON IT You can't start a debate with every person on the planet who disagrees with this crucial Christian message. But who needs to know what you learned today? How are you planning to talk up this truth?

DIG ON Read Isaiah 53 for more on what Jesus—and Jesus alone—has done for you.

9. Back From the Dead
Did Jesus actually rise from the dead?

"How can you be so gullible?" Rick sneered at David, who had just shared what he thought was the whopper reason Rick should become a Christian—the fact that Jesus rose from the dead. "Jesus was a good man—a great teacher. But last time I checked, dead bodies don't come back to life. Face it. *Poof*—he's gone! You've been swallowing a stupid myth."

BRAIN DRAIN Why do you believe Jesus really rose from the dead—or not?

FLASHBACK As new as arguments *against* the Resurrection might sound to you, they've all been used before—and rebutted. The Bible plainly claims Jesus didn't hang around in the grave for long. But are you an idiot to believe that claim? Here are the best objections opponents of Christianity have mustered—and some easy answers.

- *The disciples got lost and didn't find the right tomb.* Um, wouldn't lots of Jesus' enemies have been more than happy to point them in the right direction?
- *Jesus wasn't really dead—he "swooned."* Well, Jesus was nailed to a cross, had a spear thrust into his side, and got sealed in a tomb for three days. Would the person raising that objection like to test that theory personally?
- *The disciples stole the body.* This Bible Chunk says that story

spread early on. But exactly how could the cowardly disciples outfight heavily armed Roman soldiers?

BIBLE CHUNK Read Matthew 28:1–15

(1) After the Sabbath, at dawn on the first day of the week, Mary Magdalene and the other Mary went to look at the tomb.

(2) There was a violent earthquake, for an angel of the Lord came down from heaven and, going to the tomb, rolled back the stone and sat on it. (3) His appearance was like lightning, and his clothes were white as snow. (4) The guards were so afraid of him that they shook and became like dead men.

(5) The angel said to the women, "Do not be afraid, for I know that you are looking for Jesus, who was crucified. (6) He is not here; he has risen, just as he said. Come and see the place where he lay. (7) Then go quickly and tell his disciples: 'He has risen from the dead and is going ahead of you into Galilee. There you will see him.' Now I have told you."

(8) So the women hurried away from the tomb, afraid yet filled with joy, and ran to tell his disciples. (9) Suddenly Jesus met them. "Greetings," he said. They came to him, clasped his feet and worshiped him. (10) Then Jesus said to them, "Do not be afraid. Go and tell my brothers to go to Galilee; there they will see me."

(11) While the women were on their way, some of the guards went into the city and reported to the chief priests everything that had happened. (12) When the chief priests had met with the elders and devised a plan, they gave the soldiers a large sum of money, (13) telling them, "You are to say, 'His disciples came during the night and stole him away while we were asleep.' (14) If this report gets to the governor, we will satisfy him and keep you out of trouble." (15) So the soldiers took the money and did as they were instructed. And this story has been widely circulated among the Jews to this very day.

STUFF TO KNOW Something happens to spook the guards—and it isn't the disciples battling to fetch the body of Jesus. What is it (verses 2–4)?

Was the angel there just to scare everyone? What does he say to the women (verse 5)?

What did the soldiers say about the disappearance of Jesus' body? Do you buy that (verses 13–15)?

SIDELIGHT Even if you didn't have this Bible snippet informing you that the soldiers were paid off, the idea that the disciples stole the body is ludicrous.

- The tomb was sealed by a four-thousand-pound stone. Only a whole bunch of loudly grunting disciples could re-open the tomb. It's why the women wondered, "Who will roll the stone away from the entrance of the tomb?" (Mark 16:3).
- The tomb was guarded by a contingent of wickedly fierce Roman soldiers—anywhere from four to sixteen men. Their job was to "make the tomb as secure as you know how" (Matthew 27:62–66).
- The disciples cowered before this show of force. Peter had recently been scared into denying Jesus by a servant girl (Matthew 26:66–79).

Given those facts, it's unbelievable that the disciples snuck or smashed their way into the tomb to steal the body of Jesus.

BIG QUESTIONS If the Resurrection is true, what does that say about the other miracles in the Bible—events far easier to imagine than someone rising from the dead?

INSIGHT Proving that the miracle of the Resurrection is true doesn't just make the rest of the miracle accounts of scripture easier to swallow. It beefs up your belief in the reliability of all of scripture. And the resurrection of Jesus is the centerpiece of your faith—more on that next time.

If the Resurrection is true, what do you think it proves about Jesus?

DEEP THOT If the Resurrection had never happened, you could maybe look at Jesus as just another sweet teacher. But Romans 1:4 says that "Jesus Christ our Lord was shown to be the Son of God when God powerfully raised him from the dead by means of the Holy Spirit" (NLT). The Resurrection shows that he's the one-of-a-kind Son of God.

STICKY STUFF Grab hold of the greatest news you'll ever hear—Matthew 28:5–6.

ACT ON IT For more information than you can imagine on the truth of the Resurrection, get Josh McDowell's classic *Evidence That Demands a Verdict.*

DIG ON Read more about that Roman guard—and why it was posted—in Matthew 27:62–66.

10. Bet Your Life On It
Why does it *matter* that Jesus rose again?

"I've been learning a lot in my religion class at college," Rita's older brother said with a smug mug. "You're old enough to hear this now. See, Dad and Mom and Pastor have always made a big deal that Jesus *physically* rose from the dead. But you don't have to believe that to be a Christian. My religion professor says Jesus didn't *actually* rise from the dead—not his body, anyway. It's still in a grave somewhere. But he rose in your heart. It's the *idea* that Jesus rose that's important."

BRAIN DRAIN How would you react if archaeologist dudes or dudettes dug up a body in the Middle East and somehow proved it was Jesus? Would it make any difference to you if Jesus wasn't alive?

FLASHBACK Back in Bible times, no one claimed there was still a body in the tomb where Jesus had been laid. And the excuse that the disciples stashed Jesus' body somewhere is, well, a bad excuse. The best explanation of the fact of the empty tomb is that Jesus rose from the dead as he had promised (Matthew 16:21). Some people, though, treat Jesus' resurrection like a nice car accessory—like fuzzy dice or a CD player. Without the add-on, they figure, the car of Christianity still runs. But getting rid of the Resurrection is more like misplacing the engine. . . .

BIBLE CHUNK Read 1 Corinthians 15:1–8, 12–19

(1) Now, brothers, I want to remind you of the gospel I preached to you, which you received and on which you have taken your stand. (2) By this gospel you are saved, if you hold firmly to the word I preached to you. Otherwise, you have believed in vain.

(3) For what I received I passed on to you as of first importance: that Christ died for our sins according to the Scriptures, (4) that he was buried, that he was raised on the third day according to the Scriptures, (5) and that he appeared to Peter, and then to the Twelve. (6) After that, he appeared to more than five hundred of the brothers at the same time, most of whom are still living, though some have fallen asleep. (7) Then he appeared to James, then to all the apostles, (8) and last of all he appeared to me also, as to one abnormally born.

(12) But if it is preached that Christ has been raised from the dead, how can some of you say that there is no resurrection of the dead? (13) If there is no resurrection of the dead, then not even Christ has been raised. (14) And if Christ has not been raised, our preaching is useless and so is your faith. (15) More than that, we are then found to be false witnesses about God, for we have testified about God that he raised Christ from the dead. But he did not raise him if in fact the dead are not raised. (16) For if the dead are not raised, then Christ has not been raised either. (17) And if Christ has not been raised, your faith is futile; you are still in your sins. (18) Then those also who have fallen asleep in Christ are lost. (19) If only for this life we have hope in Christ, we are to be pitied more than all men.

STUFF TO KNOW Does it sound like Paul and the folks in Corinth take their faith seriously? How do you know (verse 1)?

SIDELIGHT Fierce persecution scattered Jesus' followers (Acts 8:1–3). People don't willingly die for a lie—and the truth of the Resurrection is the best explanation for why the disciples who hid after the Cross (John 20:19) were suddenly willing to take a stand for Christ.

What is at stake if the Corinthians don't buy this "gospel" (verse 2)?

DA'SCOOP *Gospel* is Bible lingo for the *Good News* of what Jesus did on the cross. *Salvation* is the whole package of what Jesus accomplishes for you—saving you from the penalty, the power, and—in heaven—even the presence of sin.

What facts does Paul label as ultraimportant (verses 3–8)?

Draw your own conclusion: How come Paul makes such a big deal of those factoids?

INSIGHT In a few lines Paul will say *why* it matters that people saw Jesus risen from the dead. But right here he's proving the point that far more than a handful of close disciples saw the Savior. It was a major *crowd* of people—many of whom could still be called as star witnesses to the Resurrection (verse 6).

Big point: If Jesus hasn't really risen from the dead, what good is your faith (verses 14, 17)?

Bottom line: If Jesus isn't alive, are you getting a lousy deal? What does Paul think (verse 18)?

BIG QUESTION Paul claims that Christ's resurrection is an indispensable truth. Why does the Resurrection matter to you?

What good will your faith do you if the Resurrection is a lie?

SIDELIGHT First Corinthians 6:14 says that the same power that raised Christ will someday raise you from the grave. And that same resurrection power strengthens you today to be an ultradevoted follower of Jesus. In Ephesians 1:19–20 Paul wrote that "I pray that you will begin to understand the incredible greatness of his power for us who believe him. This is the same mighty power that raised Christ from the dead and seated him in the place of honor at God's right hand in the heavenly realms" (NLT).

DEEP THOT The Resurrection isn't just an abstract belief for Bible buffs to bat around; it matters to you. Without a belief in the Resurrection, you can have a nice-looking religious shell—but your faith is like an engineless car. It won't run. At all.

STICKY STUFF Remember the things Paul says are ultraimportant—1 Corinthians 15:5–6.

ACT ON IT Tell someone about the hope you have because Jesus really rose from the dead.

DIG ON Read Acts 26, where Paul explains the reality of Christ's resurrection to a Roman ruler.

Talk About It • 2

EMPATHIZE: What's going on in your life?
ENCOURAGE: How are you doing with Jesus?
EQUIP: What one truth will you take home today?

- What persuades you that Jesus was more than just another nicey-nice religious guy? (Study 6)
- If a friend wants to know about God, where are you going to tell him or her to look? Why? (Study 6)
- So you believe in Jesus. What good does that do you? Suppose you *don't* believe in Jesus. What's the consequence? (Study 7)
- The Bible says that God saves people who believe in Jesus — and that he gives them the gift of eternal life with him in heaven. How would you explain that to a friend? (Study 7)
- Does God really expect everyone to become a Christian — or are other spiritual beliefs just as good? Explain. (Study 8)
- How would you explain to a non-Christian what makes Christianity unique — and uniquely effective in making it possible for us to know God? (Study 8)
- Why do you believe Jesus really rose from the dead — or not? What's your evidence? (Study 9)
- If the Resurrection is true, what does it prove about Jesus? (Study 9)
- If Jesus hasn't really risen from the dead, what good is your faith? (Study 10)
- The apostle Paul claims that Christ's resurrection is an indispensable truth. Why does the Resurrection matter to you? (Study 10)

PART 3

SCRUBBING UP SIN

(11.) Holier Than Thou
Does being good get you into heaven?

"I feel totally guilty around my friend," Becka confessed. "She's a Buddhist—and she's a lot more spiritual than I am, even though I'm a Christian. She thinks about her religion all the time. She listens to her parents better. She's a really good person. People even like her more. It makes me feel like a spiritual idiot. So what good is it doing me to be a Christian?"

BRAIN DRAIN How do you explain the fact that some people who don't follow Jesus seem way more spiritual than Christians?

FLASHBACK It's not hard to glance around your world—or maybe your neighborhood—and spot people who are way better at their religion than you are at yours. They out-do you in devotion, compassion, and kindness—and that can either discourage you or drive you deeper in your own faith. But two thoughts: For one, maybe they've put more effort into mastering their faith than you have into yours. For two, being good isn't what ensures you have a bona fide relationship with God. Looking spiritual, in other words, isn't the same thing as living close to God. Here's why:

BIBLE CHUNK Read Romans 3:10–25

(10) As it is written:
"There is no one righteous, not even one;

(11) there is no one who understands,
no one who seeks God.
(12) All have turned away,
they have together become worthless;
there is no one who does good,
not even one."
(13) "Their throats are open graves;
their tongues practice deceit."
"The poison of vipers is on their lips."
(14) "Their mouths are full of cursing and bitterness."
(15) "Their feet are swift to shed blood;
(16) ruin and misery mark their ways,
(17) and the way of peace they do not know."
(18) "There is no fear of God before their eyes."

(19) Now we know that whatever the law says, it says to those who are under the law, so that every mouth may be silenced and the whole world held accountable to God. (20) Therefore no one will be declared righteous in his sight by observing the law; rather, through the law we become conscious of sin.

(21) But now a righteousness from God, apart from law, has been made known, to which the Law and the Prophets testify. (22) This righteousness from God comes through faith in Jesus Christ to all who believe. There is no difference, (23) for all have sinned and fall short of the glory of God, (24) and are justified freely by his grace through the redemption that came by Christ Jesus. (25) God presented him as a sacrifice of atonement, through faith in his blood.

STUFF TO KNOW This Bible Chunk jumps right into some icky facts about humankind. Finish these phrases (verses 10–18).

- There is _____

- There is no one who _____

- No one _____

- All have _____

- We have become _____

- No one does _____

- Their throats _____

- Their tongues _____

- Their mouths _____

- There is no _____

All human beings are "under the law"—subject to God's rules. What do all those rules do for you (verses 19–20)?

Following all of God's rules *can't* do something for you. What is it (verses 19–20)?

SIDELIGHT Stumped? Rules can't make you look good before God. Paul goes on to say that you have nothing to brag about—because you can't get right with God by acting good (Romans 3:28). Being a good person—even loving others and wildly devoting yourself to following the teachings of a religion—isn't what makes you acceptable to God.

So what *does* make people friends with God (verses 22, 24)?

DA'SCOOP That's some huge language for one of the hugest concepts in the Bible. *Justification* means God declaring you "Not guilty!" You are justified by faith—made right with God through trusting in his death on your behalf. You can't save up goodie-goodie points to get into heaven. Remember? It's a free gift (Ephesians 2:8–9).

BIG QUESTIONS If being good doesn't impress God, why bother to behave?

SIDELIGHT "Christ died for all," Paul explains, "so that those who live would not continue to live for themselves. He died for them and was raised from the dead so that they would live for him" (2 Corinthians 5:15 NCV). The Jesus who gave himself for you is worth loving with your whole life.

So how do you respond to the follower of another religion who looks more spiritual than you?

DEEP THOT As good as some people look on the outside, it's impossible for any of us to match God's perfection. Compared to him, we all fall short. It's good to be good. It's better to know God. And a real relationship with God happens through Jesus.

STICKY STUFF Grab hold of God's Good News in Romans 3:23–24.

ACT ON IT Make a list of all the things you've done that you think impress God. Then tear it up—and say thanks to God for sending Jesus to make you right with him.

DIG ON Check out Galatians 1:1–10 to see how important this whole point of how you can get right with God is to Paul.

12. Going Ballistic
How can God exist when the world is so evil?

Marcus had moved to town in second grade—and ever since, he had been picked on, left out, and rubbed into the dirt. One day Marcus retaliated by bringing a gun to school. Shooting at random, he killed two kids dead and wounded a dozen more. Plenty of people wondered why God didn't stop the killing.

BRAIN DRAIN What's up with God when such ugly stuff happens? Where is he?

FLASHBACK It shouldn't shock you that people blame God for evil. They argue that if God is powerful, then he must not be too kind—or he would step in and stomp evil. If he's totally kind, then he must not be powerful—because no truly potent God would stand by while evil goes on a rampage. But before we blame God, we need to figure out where evil came from.

BIBLE CHUNK Read Romans 5:12–20 (NLT)

(12) When Adam sinned, sin entered the entire human race. Adam's sin brought death, so death spread to everyone, for everyone sinned. (13) Yes, people sinned even before the law was given. And though there was no law to break, since it had not yet been given, (14) they all died anyway— even though they did not disobey an explicit commandment of God, as Adam did. What a contrast between Adam and Christ, who was yet to come! (15) And what a difference between our sin and God's generous gift of forgiveness. For this one man, Adam, brought death to many through

his sin. But this other man, Jesus Christ, brought forgiveness to many through God's bountiful gift. (16) And the result of God's gracious gift is very different from the result of that one man's sin. For Adam's sin led to condemnation, but we have the free gift of being accepted by God, even though we are guilty of many sins. (17) The sin of this one man, Adam, caused death to rule over us, but all who receive God's wonderful, gracious gift of righteousness will live in triumph over sin and death through this one man, Jesus Christ.

(18) Yes, Adam's one sin brought condemnation upon everyone, but Christ's one act of righteousness makes all people right in God's sight and gives them life. (19) Because one person disobeyed God, many people became sinners. But because one other person obeyed God, many people will be made right in God's sight.

(20) God's law was given so that all people could see how sinful they were. But as people sinned more and more, God's wonderful kindness became more abundant. (21) So just as sin ruled over all people and brought them to death, now God's wonderful kindness rules instead, giving us right standing with God and resulting in eternal life through Jesus Christ our Lord.

STUFF TO KNOW What happened when Adam munched that apple way back in the Garden of Eden—what "entered the entire human race" (verse 12)?

What did Adam's sin bring to everyone (verse 12)?

Why did death spread to everyone (verse 12)?

SIDELIGHT The Bible argues that death spread to everyone because everyone sinned. A sin affects not just people but *all of creation*—which explains why mosquitoes suck blood and tornados blow down homes. Romans 8:20 says that sin

undid the harmony God intended for your world—and Romans 8:21 says that "All creation anticipates the day when it will join God's children in glorious freedom from death and decay" (Romans 8:21 NLT).

Paul's next point is this: God spelled out a bunch of rules *after* people had rebelled against him (verses 13–14). God could have smacked us. But what gift does he give us instead (verse 15)?

If Adam infected the human race with the nasty disease of death, what good thing did Jesus do (verses 16–18)?

BIG QUESTIONS So who do you think is responsible for the world's evil? Why?

INSIGHT The Bible says Adam was responsible for the start of evil. Even if that's hard for you or your non-Christian friends to swallow, you still have to reckon with this: Each one of us is undeniably responsible for its spread.

Okay—so even if you accept that people are to blame for the world's trouble, then why doesn't God step in and stop evil?

SIDELIGHT He did. Even when human beings hated God, he sent Jesus to win us forgiveness and new life—a far

better alternative than taking away our freedom to choose or snuffing us out altogether. Jesus struck a fatal blow at Satan and the forces of evil (Colossians 1:15), but it's up to each of us to choose to participate in his plan.

Why doesn't God punish evildoers right away—as in last week?

SIDELIGHT Hmmm . . . would you like God to rapidly punish everything bad you do? God has promised to squash evil, but his plan is built on patience: "The Lord is not slow in doing what he promised—the way some people understand slowness. But God is being patient with you. He does not want anyone to be lost. But he wants everyone to change their heart and life" (2 Peter 3:9 NCV). God gives us time to come to him.

DEEP THOT Most people who blame God for evil are way less concerned about acknowledging their own guilt and fixing their own behavior than they are about blaming God—the one who has done everything possible to stomp out evil short of stomping out the human race.

STICKY STUFF Romans 5:17 says where sin comes from—and tells you God's solution.

ACT ON IT What are you going to do today to stop sin in your own life?

DIG ON Have a look at Galatians 6:7–9, which promises that you reap what you sow.

13. Back at Ya, Bubba
Are Christians wimps?

Ever since Lindsey became a Christian she'd had to fight the teasing of her hardcore soccer teammates. So when her coach gave his annual pre-tryout peptalk—*there's no room for sugar and spice or anything nice on this team . . . I need some girls who will kick some backside . . . and kick it hard*—she got ready to get ripped. Sure enough, Edie raised her hand and smiled. "Coach, Lindsey can't do that. She's a Christian."

BRAIN DRAIN So are Christians a herd of wimps? What's your evidence?

FLASHBACK You want weak? You got it. The heart of Christianity is admitting you need help. After all, Jesus said his followers need help: "Healthy people don't need a doctor—sick people do. I have come to call sinners to turn from their sins, not to spend my time with those who think they are already good enough" (Luke 5:31–32 NLT). But get this: That hefty hunk of honest humility doesn't make Christians weak. They can play a fair but tough game of ball—or go nose-to-nose in the business world or battlefield.

The start of this Bible Chunk refers to "they," a bunch of people who claim to be more spiritual than Paul. He blasts back at their criticism—and proves just how tough Christians can be.

BIBLE CHUNK Read 2 Corinthians 11:23–29

(23) Are they servants of Christ? (I am out of my mind to talk like this.) I am more. I have worked much harder, been in prison more frequently, been flogged more severely, and been exposed to death again and again. (24) Five times I received from the Jews the forty lashes minus one. (25) Three times I was beaten with rods, once I was stoned, three times I was shipwrecked, I spent a night and a day in the open sea, (26) I have been constantly on the move. I have been in danger from rivers, in danger from bandits, in danger from my own countrymen, in danger from Gentiles; in danger in the city, in danger in the country, in danger at sea; and in danger from false brothers. (27) I have labored and toiled and have often gone without sleep; I have known hunger and thirst and have often gone without food; I have been cold and naked. (28) Besides everything else, I face daily the pressure of my concern for all the churches. (29) Who is weak, and I do not feel weak? Who is led into sin, and I do not inwardly burn?

STUFF TO KNOW Next time you hear someone moan that Christians are all hyperprotected Mamma's boys— and Daddy's girls—just ponder Paul's life. What all has he been through (verses 23–28)? Jot a list!

You get the picture: Paul faced terrible outside suffering. What was going on inside? What other pressure did he feel (verses 28–29)?

What do you think Paul meant by the pressure he felt for the church (verses 28–29)?

SIDELIGHT God gave Paul the responsibility of spreading the Good News of Jesus—and overseeing the health of growing churches. Acts 20:18–21 and 28–31 shows some of the pressure he felt.

Make a guess: Is Paul the only follower of Jesus to have suffered like that?

SIDELIGHT Paul isn't the only believer to have suffered for his faith. Check this list from the Bible book of Hebrews: "Others were tortured. . . . Some faced jeers and flogging, while still others were chained and put in prison. They were stoned; they were sawed in two; they were put to death by the sword. They went about in sheepskins and goatskins, destitute, persecuted and mistreated. . . . They wandered in deserts and mountains, and in caves and holes in the ground" (Hebrews 11:35–38).

BIG QUESTIONS So does Paul sound like a wuss?

If you had been sawed in two for your faith, no one would doubt your toughness. Since you're still in one piece, how can you prove your faith doesn't make you a wimp?

SIDELIGHT Sooner or later, suffering becomes a part of every Christian's faith—whether the pain of persecution or the sting of staying obedient. Paul once wrote, "For you have been given not only the privilege of trusting in Christ but also the privilege of suffering for him" (Philippians 1:29 NLT).

Agree or disagree: The wimpiest way to get through life is to go along with the crowd and give in to sin.

SIDELIGHT Jesus said it straight: Going God's way is the toughest choice you can make. "You can enter God's Kingdom only through the narrow gate," he said. "The highway to hell is broad, and its gate is wide for the many who choose the easy way. But the gateway to life is small, and the road is narrow, and only a few ever find it" (Matthew 7:13–14 NLT).

DEEP THOT Christians get squeezed by pressures inside and out. If you still wonder if Christians are wimps, get another dose of Paul in 1 Corinthians 9:24–27—and ask God to toughen you up!

STICKY STUFF Hang tough with the truth of Philippians 1:29.

ACT ON IT Read Matthew 5:44—then pray for someone who gives you a tough time for following Jesus.

DIG ON Read Peter's encouragement to Christians who suffer in 1 Peter 1:3–9; 4:12–19.

(14.) Dead People's Bones
Why are some Christians hypocrites?

The old ladies at church said Becka sang like an angel. But any student at school could tell you that on Friday and Saturday nights she drank like a fish. Every Sunday morning at worship services she *tra-la-la'd* about God's greatness. But every weekend her actions sang a totally different song.

BRAIN DRAIN No one has anything nice to say about hypocrites. So what exactly is a hypocrite?

FLASHBACK If you read that last Bible Chunk and still wonder if Christians are weak, here's another passage to silence that creepy *Christians-are-wussies* worry. You'll see that Jesus could do more than suffer through the ugly stuff people tossed at him—he can dish it out, too. And look hard at who Jesus picks as his target. It's the Pharisees—the religious show-offs of Bible times. His words are a top-ten list of things he hates about hypocrites.

BIBLE CHUNK Read Matthew 23:1–15, 27–28 (NLT)

(1) Then Jesus said to the crowds and to his disciples, (2) "The teachers of religious law and the Pharisees are the official interpreters of the Scriptures. (3) So practice and obey whatever they say to you, but don't follow their example. For they don't practice what they teach. (4) They crush you with impossible religious demands and never lift a finger to help ease the burden.

(5) "Everything they do is for show. On their arms they wear extra wide

prayer boxes with Scripture verses inside, and they wear extra long tassels on their robes. (6) And how they love to sit at the head table at banquets and in the most prominent seats in the synagogue! (7) They enjoy the attention they get on the streets, and they enjoy being called 'Rabbi.' (8) Don't ever let anyone call you 'Rabbi,' for you have only one teacher, and all of you are on the same level as brothers and sisters. (9) And don't address anyone here on earth as 'Father,' for only God in heaven is your spiritual Father. (10) And don't let anyone call you 'Master,' for there is only one master, the Messiah. (11) The greatest among you must be a servant. (12) But those who exalt themselves will be humbled, and those who humble themselves will be exalted.

(13) "How terrible it will be for you teachers of religious law and you Pharisees. Hypocrites! For you won't let others enter the Kingdom of Heaven, and you won't go in yourselves. (15) Yes, how terrible it will be for you teachers of religious law and you Pharisees. For you cross land and sea to make one convert, and then you turn him into twice the son of hell as you yourselves are.

(27) "How terrible it will be for you teachers of religious law and you Pharisees. Hypocrites! You are like whitewashed tombs—beautiful on the outside but filled on the inside with dead people's bones and all sorts of impurity. (28) You try to look like upright people outwardly, but inside your hearts are filled with hypocrisy and lawlessness."

STUFF TO KNOW Who exactly does Jesus aim this blast at (verses 1–2)?

Do the Pharisees follow their own rules (verse 3)? What do they do instead (verse 4)?

Ouch: Jesus rattles off some reasons the Pharisees do what they do. What are they? Jot down a few of Jesus' sharp points from verses 5–7.

INSIGHT The Pharisees accessorized their clothing with *prayer boxes* and *long tassels*, both symbols of their spirituality. The *synagogue* was a local center of worship, and *rabbi* meant "my master" or "my teacher."

How does Jesus coach you to act (verses 8–10)? How does he want you to think about yourself (verses 11–12)?

Double ouch: So how happy is Jesus about how the Pharisees act? Can hypocrites like the Pharisees expect to get into heaven (verses 13–15)?

What else does Jesus call the Pharisees (verse 27)? What's he mean by that (verse 28)?

BIG QUESTIONS So after reading all that, how would you define "hypocrite"?

DA'SCOOP The word *hypocrite* means "mask," as in the masks Greek actors wore to pretend to be something they weren't. So Jesus isn't slamming sincere but imperfect followers; he's aiming at persistent religious fakes, those who claim to live close to God but don't.

Should God get the blame for how hypocrites act?

How do you think God will handle hypocrites?

SIDELIGHT God is far more angry about hypocrites than any human can ever be. Right after the chunk you read, Jesus ends his chat with the warning, "Snakes! Sons of vipers! How will you escape the judgment of hell?" (Matthew 23:33 NLT). But James 4:7–10 and Matthew 7:3–5 tell how they can get right with him.

DEEP THOT Before you run out and get heated at your most-disliked hypocrite, know that God gets really hot if you point fingers at others when you have the same problem. "Examine yourselves," says 2 Corinthians 13:5, "to see if your faith is really genuine" (NLT). And let God handle the hypocrites.

STICKY STUFF Matthew 23:27–28 will help you remember what hypocrisy looks like.

ACT ON IT If you've acted hypocritically, get that straight with God—and with the humans you hurt.

DIG ON Find out more about what hypocrisy looks like in Isaiah 29:13–14. And find out why God doesn't smoke them right away in Matthew 13:24–30, 36–43.

15. Ta-Dah
Why do Christians always tell people about God?

Marc yanked a tarp off his latest invention. "It's a Gospel Golf-cart," he said with glee. "It's my best invention yet for telling the world about Jesus. It's a fifty-thousand-watt sound system mounted on a five-thousand-horsepower cart. The harder I press the gas pedal, the louder it plays a hymn. It goes on-road or off. I can talk over traffic—and you should see the faces at the golf course when I break into an evangelistic sermon during someone's backswing!"

BRAIN DRAIN Have you ever gotten in someone's face about your faith? What happened? If not, are you flawlessly nice—or do you never talk about your faith?

FLASHBACK You probably know that you should share your faith—because you're supposed to. After all, Jesus told his followers to "go and make followers of all people in the world" (Matthew 28:19 NCV). But talking about Jesus is more than a must-do. Jesus compared finding God to discovering a hugely expensive pearl—one worth giving your whole life to get (Matthew 13:45–46). And this is one treasure too big to hog for yourself.

BIBLE CHUNK Read 1 Peter 3:13–18

(13) Who is going to harm you if you are eager to do good? (14) But even if you should suffer for what is right, you are blessed. "Do not fear

what they fear; do not be frightened." (15) But in your hearts set apart Christ as Lord. Always be prepared to give an answer to everyone who asks you to give the reason for the hope that you have. But do this with gentleness and respect, (16) keeping a clear conscience, so that those who speak maliciously against your good behavior in Christ may be ashamed of their slander. (17) It is better, if it is God's will, to suffer for doing good than for doing evil. (18) For Christ died for sins once for all, the righteous for the unrighteous, to bring you to God.

STUFF TO KNOW What kind of treatment do you usually expect when you work hard to do what's right (verse 13)?

Well, Jesus did right and died for it. How should you feel when you do well and get whacked (verse 14)?

INSIGHT Wonder where the "they" in verse 14 came from? It's a quote from Isaiah 8:12–13. The simple meaning is "So don't be afraid and don't worry."

So whatcha supposed to do instead of getting scared—who should you let run your life (verse 15)?

Here's where this Bible Chunk gets specific about sharing Jesus. How can you respond to people who wonder about your faith (verse 15)?

- Who are you obeying when you get psyched up to share?

- What should you be ready for?

- You should sass people who question you and act like they're stupid, right? Actually—how should you speak?

INSIGHT Not a lot of people bug you with bluntly biblical questions like "What must I do to be saved?" (Acts 16:30). The words someone uses to tell you they want to know about Jesus come out sounding different—like "Why are you different from everyone else?" or "Why do you go to church?" And sometimes their sharing a struggle can be a signal they're ready for you to speak up.

What good will that do you to "keep a clear conscience" (verse 16)? What's that mean?

Sharing respectfully, wisely, and without hypocrisy still sometimes brings you grief. How can you keep cool (verses 17–18)?

SIDELIGHT You can start by pondering the price Jesus paid. He thought the goal of bringing people to God was so great he was willing to die for it. A chapter before this chunk, the Bible says that "When they hurled their insults at him, he did not retaliate . . . by his wounds you have been healed" (1 Peter 2:23–24).

BIG QUESTIONS How would you want someone to talk to you about God?

Why don't Christians just keep quiet—and let other people believe what they want?

How would you answer someone who says Christians are always "shoving their faith down other people's throats"?

INSIGHT Your best answer is your own story—being able to say you talk about Jesus "with gentleness and respect." And it doesn't hurt to explain what the Bible says in this chunk about how *God* says you should spread his Good News.

DEEP THOT If what the Bible says is true, choosing *not* to tell others about Jesus isn't an option.

STICKY STUFF Make it your goal to share Jesus the way the Bible says. Memorize 1 Peter 3:15.

ACT ON IT Think of someone who would be surprised by the compassion in this command. Explain what it says—and ask what he or she thinks.

DIG ON Look at Acts 6:8; 8:2 to see the calm way Stephen explained God's Good News to a hostile mob.

Talk About It • 3

EMPATHIZE: What's going on in your life?
ENCOURAGE: How are you doing with Jesus?
EQUIP: What one truth will you take home today?

- How do you explain the fact that some people who don't follow Jesus seem way more spiritual than Christians? (Study 11)
- Following all of God's rules *can't* do something for you. What? (Study 11)
- So what makes people friends with God? (Study 11)
- Where is God when ugly stuff happens to good people? (Study 12)
- Who do you think is responsible for the world's evil? Why? (Study 12)
- How would you answer someone who thinks all Christians are wimps? (Study 13)
- Agree or disagree: The wimpiest way to get through life is to go along with the crowd and give in to sin. (Study 13)
- What's a hypocrite? Should God get the blame for how hypocrites act? Should Christians be blamed for the bad way some Christians act? (Study 14)
- How will God handle hypocrites? Do you think that's fair— or not? (Study 14)
- Are you ever a hypocrite? What should God do with you? (Study 14)
- Do you never talk about your faith? Why—or why not? (Study 15)
- Why don't Christians just keep quiet—and let other people believe what they want? (Study 15)
- How would you answer someone who says Christians are always "shoving their faith down other people's throats"? (Study 15)

PART 4

GRABBING GOD'S BEST

16. Sleephair
Why doesn't God answer all my prayers?

For months Maria prayed for her grandma—whenever she thought of it, in fact, which was all the time. As her grandma's cancer continued to spread, Maria kept praying, sure that God would rescue her grandma and heal her. So when her grandma died in her sleep one night, Maria was shattered. "It's hard to believe in God anymore," she says. "I prayed and he didn't answer."

BRAIN DRAIN What do you expect to happen when you pray?

FLASHBACK Maybe you think God is a cruel grouch—the kind of guy who doesn't want you to pester him with your requests. But maybe you know Jesus said to ask for what you want—and promised his Father would answer (Matthew 18:19). Or that the Bible even says that sometimes you don't have what you want because you haven't asked God for it (James 4:2 NLT). So what's up when you pray and nothing happens?

BIBLE CHUNK Read Luke 11:5–13

(5) Then he [Jesus] said to them, "Suppose one of you has a friend, and he goes to him at midnight and says, 'Friend, lend me three loaves of bread, (6) because a friend of mine on a journey has come to me, and I have nothing to set before him.'

(7) "Then the one inside answers, 'Don't bother me. The door is already locked, and my children are with me in bed. I can't get up and give you

anything.' (8) I tell you, though he will not get up and give him the bread because he is his friend, yet because of the man's persistence he will get up and give him as much as he needs.

(9) "So I say to you: Ask and it will be given to you; seek and you will find; knock and the door will be opened to you. (10) For everyone who asks receives; he who seeks finds; and to him who knocks, the door will be opened.

(11) "Which of you fathers, if your son asks for a fish, will give him a snake instead? (12) Or if he asks for an egg, will give him a scorpion? (13) If you then, though you are evil, know how to give good gifts to your children, how much more will your Father in heaven give the Holy Spirit to those who ask him!"

STUFF TO KNOW Think hard: Is Jesus comparing God to the grouch who doesn't want to get out of bed? How would that make God look (verse 7)?

What makes Mr. Dozing Friend finally get up and give in (verse 9)?

What do you suppose that says about how you should make requests to God (verse 8)?

INSIGHT Get this: Jesus just finished teaching his followers the words you know as the Lord's Prayer, where he makes it totally clear that God is *glad* to give. So Jesus is *contrasting* the grouch to God, not saying God is *like* the grouch. This parable is also less about God than about us. God's big goal in you is to build trust—persistent trust that keeps asking and keeps believing in God's total goodness to you. That's the first thing he wants you to get out of prayer. And it's even more important

than any great thing you could get.

What can you count on God to *always* give you (verse 10)?

SIDELIGHT Jesus makes the same point here that
James makes toward the back of the Bible: God only knows
how to give *great* gifts: "Every good and perfect gift is from
above," James says. And, he notes, God's commitment to do
you good never changes (James 1:17).

So what exactly does God promise to give you if you ask
(verse 13)?

INSIGHT Ferraris! JetSkis! Jacuzzis! That's what pops to
the top of the lists of goodies humans want from God. But the
gift God is most ready to give is *himself*.

BIG QUESTIONS When have *you* prayed—not gotten what you wanted—and felt grossly disappointed?

Why don't you get an answer to every prayer?

INSIGHT Actually, you *always* get an answer—just not the
answer you expect. When God hears your prayers, he has at
least three options in answering: "yes," "no," or "not now."

If God's goal is to teach you to trust him—to believe that he's good and always wants what's best for you, how can you respond to those "nos" and "not nows"?

Is there a guaranteed way to get what you ask for every time? Explain.

SIDELIGHT First John 5:14–15 says you can be confident about getting your request under one crucial condition— that you ask according to God's will. Big meaning: *Ask for what you believe to be good, but let God pick what's best.*

How would you explain all this to a friend who's hurting because God didn't give what he or she wanted?

DEEP THOT God is no sleephaired monster who rolls over, pulls the blanket tight, and stuffs a pillow in his ears. He has more wisdom than you can fathom. And he's too good to give in to every silly whim—or even to grant your every deep wish. For more on understanding prayer, check the ETD book *Pray Hard.* In the meantime, your first job is to trust God—even when you don't understand his answers.

STICKY STUFF Remember that God wants you to *ask*: Luke 11:9–10.

ACT ON IT Talk about it with a mature Christian friend: How has God answered your prayers?

DIG ON See for yourself what 1 John 5:14–15 says.

(17.) Little Miss Evil
Does God want to spoil my fun?

"Why would anyone want to be a Christian?" Brandi snapped. "If you're a Christian, you can't do anything. I mean, it's not like I want to be totally evil. I'm not going to rob convenience stores or run over small animals or anything. But isn't trying stuff what high school is all about? I think God is like my rule-making mother on steroids. He's, like, out to dismember my life. Girls just want to have fun."

BRAIN DRAIN Why do you suppose God makes rules?

FLASHBACK If you want to load up on God's rules for life, this next chunk offers a bunch. It's part of Jesus' most famous hunk of teaching—so famous it has its own name, the "Sermon on the Mount." It starts with the Beatitudes, where Jesus explains how you can get truly happy (Matthew 5:1–12). Then he details God's commands for standing out from the world (5:13–16), handling anger (5:21–26), sex (5:27–32), dealing with enemies (5:38–48), prayer (6:5–15 and 7:7–12), not stuffing yourself with stuff (6:19–24), and judging (7:1–5). But if you're worried that Jesus lays down the law just to undo your fun, check what he says next.

BIBLE CHUNK Read Matthew 7:24–27

(24) "Therefore everyone who hears these words of mine and puts them into practice is like a wise man who built his house on the rock.

(25) The rain came down, the streams rose, and the winds blew and beat against that house; yet it did not fall, because it had its foundation on the rock. (26) But everyone who hears these words of mine and does not put them into practice is like a foolish man who built his house on sand. (27) The rain came down, the streams rose, and the winds blew and beat against that house, and it fell with a great crash."

STUFF TO KNOW What does Jesus want you to do with his words (verse 24)?

So if you follow those instructions, what are you (verse 24)?

Explain what happens to the wise guy in this Bible Chunk (verse 25).

What makes the other guy an idiot (verse 26)?

What happens to that not-so-smart guy (verses 26–27)?

SIDELIGHT Face it: Anyone with one eyeball can see that bad girls and guys often win in this world. And you might wonder if evildoers will always get away with wickedness. People in the Bible puzzled over that one too—but only until they saw what God has planned. Check this Old Testament

Bible Chunk: "Then one day I went into your sanctuary, O God, and I thought about the destiny of the wicked. Truly, you put them on a slippery path and send them sliding over the cliff to destruction. In an instant they are destroyed, swept away by terrors. Their present life is only a dream that is gone when they awake. When you arise, O Lord, you will make them vanish from this life" (Psalm 73:17–20 NLT).

BIG QUESTIONS You see two guys in this story. Which one do you think ends up happier? Why?

Let's figure that the guy who built on the beach was having a whole heap of fun until God came along and kicked over his sand castle. Wouldn't it be better to have gotten in on his fun? Why—or why not?

INSIGHT Ponder this: Lots of times the fun that humans long for is like wanting to slam your hand in a car door a few times before your parents catch you. And get this: Nothing God forbids is fun *in the long run* for *all people affected.*

How is it possible to hear God's words and not put them into practice? What does that look like?

What do you think is the right-here-right-now payoff for obeying God—putting his words into practice?

SIDELIGHT

SIDELIGHT John 14:23 says that when you choose to obey God's rules, it results in a cool closeness with him. He said this: "All those who love me will do what I say. My Father will love them, and we will come to them and live with them" (NLT).

Get honest: Are you glad God spells out right and wrong for your life—or not? How come?

INSIGHT

INSIGHT Think about this: God is totally mighty, caring, and smart. He's Ultimate Power, so he could force you to obey his commands. But he's also Ultimate Love and Ultimate Intelligence. And that makes him worth obeying with your whole life.

Would you guess that most people on this planet are wise—or wacko? Based on what evidence?

DEEP THOT

DEEP THOT Right before this Bible Chunk Jesus hands you the answer—and he says where folks who only ignore God's commands are headed. Have another look at Matthew 7:13–14, a chunk you saw a few pages back in Study 13.

STICKY STUFF

STICKY STUFF Matthew 7:24 will help you walk on the wise side.

ACT ON IT

ACT ON IT Make a list of bad things you've thought about trying—and add to your list God's good reasons not to.

DIG ON

DIG ON Dig into Psalm 73 for a deep explanation of the fate of people who think they can get away with all sorts of evil.

18. Mr. Crusty
Aren't God's rules out-of-date?

The apostle Paul didn't face the pressure of an all-night prom party. Jesus grew up in an out-of-the-way town in old-time Israel. Neither of those guys lived online. They weren't pummeled twenty-four/seven by advertisers and spinmeisters. They didn't arrive home to absentee parents or face a future where only the eggheadedly smart survive. If they knew nothing about safe sex or designer drugs or any of this other stuff, how could they know what good or evil or temptation is really about? How could they ever carve out rules that fit *your* life?

BRAIN DRAIN Do you think God is a crusty old guy in the sky—and that his rules for living are too obnoxiously dated to bother following? Explain.

FLASHBACK You don't have to read far into the Old Testament to see that people were into evil way past PG-13— from child sacrifice to idol worship, incest, and witchcraft. Life wasn't any prettier in the New Testament. Paul writes about "the sexually immoral ... idolaters ... adulterers ... male prostitutes ... homosexual offenders ... thieves ... the greedy ... drunkards ... slanderers ... swindlers" and reminds his readers "that is what some of you were" (1 Corinthians 6:9–11). God knows how grotesque evil can get. And you can be sure that he set up his rules for your real world.

BIBLE CHUNK Read 2 Corinthians 6:14–7:1 (NLT)

(14) Don't team up with those who are unbelievers. How can goodness be a partner with wickedness? How can light live with darkness? (15) What harmony can there be between Christ and the Devil? How can a believer be a partner with an unbeliever? (16) And what union can there be between God's temple and idols? For we are the temple of the living God. As God said:

"I will live in them
and walk among them.
I will be their God,
and they will be my people.
(17)Therefore, come out from them
and separate yourselves from them, says the Lord.
Don't touch their filthy things,
and I will welcome you.
(18) And I will be your Father,
and you will be my sons and daughters,
says the Lord Almighty."

(7:1) Because we have these promises, dear friends, let us cleanse ourselves from everything that can defile our body or spirit. And let us work toward complete purity because we fear God.

STUFF TO KNOW First off, are you surprised by the evil that people were into back in Bible times? How come?

The start of this Bible Chunk tells believers not to "team up" with unbelievers. Why not? Who are you already connected to (verses 6:14–15)?

DA'SCOOP That term "team up" is actually "yoked," a farming term for lashing two animals together to make them hoe the same row. The point of this Bible Chunk isn't that you should cut yourself off from all non-Christians. It's warning you

against partnerships that drag you into sin.

In verse 6:16 God promises to stick close to you. What does he want from you in return (verse 6:17)?

And what will you enjoy if you do that (verse 6:18)?

INSIGHT Obeying God's rules doesn't make you his child, but it lets you live close to him. When you think how he thinks and act how he acts, that's following. You go where he goes.

What are you supposed to do—and try to do totally? Why (verse 7:1)?

DA'SCOOP *Body and spirit* means getting your complete person completely clean—inside and out, in how you get along with both God and people. *Fear,* by the way, isn't raw fright. It's reverence and respect—obeying out of awe for God.

BIG QUESTIONS So does it sound like God understood your world when he laid down a Bible full of do's and don'ts? Explain.

SIDELIGHT You might not be satisfied that God looked

at planet earth and saw a whole heap of sin going on. The Bible also tells us that Jesus knows firsthand the pressures you face: Jesus was "tempted in every way, just as we are—yet was without sin" (Hebrews 4:15). Christ's sinlessness doesn't mean his life was temptationless.

Do you think God's commands still fit your world today? Why—or why not?

INSIGHT God saw sin clearly enough—and thought it was bad enough—to send his Son to die for the world's evil. He made his rules knowing exactly what a bad world was like—and knowing perfectly what a good world could be. Think about this: *God understands evil better than you ever can because he understands goodness better than you ever will.*

DEEP THOT Jesus is the guy who noticed that Satan's goal is to "steal and kill and destroy." God's purpose "is to give life in all its fullness" (John 10:10 NLT). Sounds like God is the one who knows what real fun is all about.

STICKY STUFF Stuff one of God's smartest rules for life into your head: 2 Corinthians 6:14.

ACT ON IT Talk with a mature Christian about how wanting the wrong kinds of fun and friends might be dragging you down.

DIG ON Grab a look at Ephesians 4:17–32 for more on what God knows about evil—and about good.

19. Hide-and-Seek
Is God out to get me?

You dart behind a tree, turning sideways to get skinny, scared to throw the slightest shadow. See, God is chasing you down. He's got a cowboy hat—and a four-wheel-drive pickup—with a loaded gun rack—and a searchlight to shine into your life and spot your sin. You settle down for a long stay—and pray you don't get caught.

BRAIN DRAIN Do you ever worry that God wants to hunt you down and hurt you? How come you do—or don't?

FLASHBACK Some Bible-bashers paint God as the Godzilla of the universe, the guy who wants to rip you limb from limb for your sin. They need a lesson from the Bible. Yes, God is the "righteous Judge" (2 Timothy 4:8), and like Jesus said, he's the one who can "destroy both soul and body in hell" (Matthew 10:28). But God wants to be friends with anyone who allows him in (Revelation 3:20), and his greatest goal is for the whole world to know him (2 Peter 3:9). This Bible chunk by David is a fresh look at what some folks call the dreaded "Old Testament God of Wrath."

BIBLE CHUNK Read Psalm 103:1–19

(1) Praise the Lord, O my soul;
   all my inmost being, praise his holy name.
(2) Praise the Lord, O my soul,

and forget not all his benefits.
(3) He forgives all my sins
and heals all my diseases;
(4) he redeems my life from the pit
and crowns me with love and compassion.
(5) He satisfies my desires with good things,
so that my youth is renewed like the eagle's.
(6) The Lord works righteousness
and justice for all the oppressed.
(7) He made known his ways to Moses,
his deeds to the people of Israel:
(8) The Lord is compassionate and gracious,
slow to anger, abounding in love.
(9) He will not always accuse,
nor will he harbor his anger forever;
(10) he does not treat us as our sins deserve
or repay us according to our iniquities.
(11) For as high as the heavens are above the earth,
so great is his love for those who fear him;
(12) as far as the east is from the west,
so far has he removed our transgressions from us.
(13) As a father has compassion on his children,
so the Lord has compassion on those who fear him;
(14) for he knows how we are formed,
he remembers that we are dust.
(15) As for man, his days are like grass,
he flourishes like a flower of the field;
(16) the wind blows over it and it is gone,
and its place remembers it no more.
(17) But from everlasting to everlasting
the Lord's love is with those who fear him,
and his righteousness with their children's children—
(18) with those who keep his covenant
and remember to obey his precepts.
(19) The Lord has established his throne in heaven,
and his kingdom rules over all.

STUFF TO KNOW Right away David says he's
going to praise God for the good stuff he brings (verse 2). Name
six things God does (verses 3–5).

Find two more things he does—this time in verses 6–7.

So what motivates God to do all this? What's he like (verse 8)?

Okay. This next section fesses up to the fact that every human alive does wrong. Big question: Do you get what you deserve (verse 10)?

SIDELIGHT God called David "a man after my own heart" (Acts 13:22). Yet if you read Psalm 51, you discover David had some major sins to straighten out with God. The point? You can trust David's first-hand scoop on God's forgiveness.

What's God do with your sin (verse 12)?

SIDELIGHT Spot that? God tosses your sins as far as he can fling them. First John 2:2 says that Jesus has died for all people. But all people still need to grab hold of the awesome effects of his death through faith.

BIG QUESTIONS How come God looks at you with compassion? (Hint: Have a look at verses 14–16.)

SIDELIGHT God does better than cutting you slack. Through Jesus, he gets rid of your sins completely. Isaiah 43:25 says God "blots out your sins for my own sake and will never think of them again" (NLT).

So how do you get unscared of God?

SIDELIGHT God gives you a simple way to straighten out your sins. Whether you're coming to him for the first time or you need to keep your relationship with him fresh, God wants you to admit your wrongs to him. First John 1:8–9 puts it like this: "If we say that we have no sin, we are fooling ourselves, and the truth is not in us. But if we confess our sins, he will forgive our sins. We can trust God. He does what is right. He will make us clean from all the wrongs we have done" (NCV).

DEEP THOT You can make up your own mind, but this Bible Chunk makes God sound more like he's eager to help you than to hurt you.

STICKY STUFF You could stuff that whole psalm in your brain—but at least start with 103:11–12.

ACT ON IT If you've never told God that you need his forgiveness, tell him now. And if you need to, tell him again.

DIG ON Study Psalm 19:12–14 to see how David invites God to help him spot his own sins.

20. God Who?

What is God really like?

Your stomach jumps to your throat as you stand in the thick of a religious festival. You're in India, and you gasp as you watch worshipers pierce their bodies with hundreds of hooks. Some slice daggers through their cheeks. Others put small spears through their tongues. And as you watch, one thought streaks through your mind: What kind of god do they follow?

BRAIN DRAIN Tell how you'd explain it to a non-Christian: Why would anyone want to be a Christian?

FLASHBACK Becoming a Christian doesn't sign you up for a religion of tedious ceremonies or gory self-mutilation. You're getting a relationship with the King of the Universe. Here's why: God's big plan is for human beings to be friends with himself and other people. Even though human beings have shredded those relationships, God is working to bring us back to an eternity of friendship in heaven. If you ever wonder what kind of God you're hanging tight to, this psalm by David gives you a good look.

BIBLE CHUNK Read Psalm 145:1–21 (NLT)

(1) I will praise you, my God and King,
and bless your name forever and ever.

(2) I will bless you every day,
   and I will praise you forever.
(3) Great is the Lord! He is most worthy of praise!
   His greatness is beyond discovery!
(4) Let each generation tell its children
   of your mighty acts.
(5) I will meditate on your majestic, glorious splendor
   and your wonderful miracles.
(6) Your awe-inspiring deeds will be on every tongue;
   I will proclaim your greatness.
(7) Everyone will share the story of your wonderful goodness;
   they will sing with joy of your righteousness.
(8) The Lord is kind and merciful,
   slow to get angry, full of unfailing love.
(9) The Lord is good to everyone.
   He showers compassion on all his creation.
(10) All of your works will thank you, Lord,
   and your faithful followers will bless you.
(11) They will talk together about the glory of your kingdom;
   they will celebrate examples of your power.
(12) They will tell about your mighty deeds
   and about the majesty and glory of your reign.
(13) For your kingdom is an everlasting kingdom.
   You rule generation after generation.
   The Lord is faithful in all he says;
   he is gracious in all he does.
(14) The Lord helps the fallen
   and lifts up those bent beneath their loads.
(15) All eyes look to you for help;
   you give them their food as they need it.
(16) When you open your hand,
   you satisfy the hunger and thirst of every living thing.
(17) The Lord is righteous in everything he does;
   he is filled with kindness.
(18) The Lord is close to all who call on him,
   yes, to all who call on him sincerely.
(19) He fulfills the desires of those who fear him;
   he hears their cries for help and rescues them.
(20) The Lord protects all those who love him,
   but he destroys the wicked.
(21) I will praise the Lord,
   and everyone on earth will bless his holy name
   forever and forever.

STUFF TO KNOW So does David sound like he's happy with God? How do you know (verses 1–2)?

What's David filling his mind and mouth with (verses 3–7)?

God is quick to get angry—and stingy with his love, right? What is he (verse 8)?

What whopper reason does David give you to praise God (verses 8–9)?

SIDELIGHT You might figure God's goodness never shows up in your life in spectacular ways. But don't ignore the good stuff he showers on his whole creation—from the miracle of breath to the warmth of the sun.

God's people are abuzz. About what (verses 10–13)?

What does God have in store for people who follow him (verses 15–19)?

BIG QUESTIONS Where do you think people get goofed-up ideas of God?

Do you think it's fair that God does great stuff for his followers—but plans punishment for anyone who rejects him?

INSIGHT God's goodness is available to anyone who wants it. Some of God's good stuff is present all the time—and comes down on people both good and bad (Matthew 5:45). Other good stuff becomes yours when you take shelter in God. It's like this: God can only rescue you if you cry to him for help.

DEEP THOT God doesn't make you bloody your body to follow him. He's got good stuff in mind for you. "I know what I have planned for you," he says. "I have good plans for you. I don't plan to hurt you. I plan to give you hope and a good future" (Jeremiah 29:11 NCV). That's the kind of God worth worshiping.

STICKY STUFF You can't find a better God to hang on to than the one you see in Psalm 145:17–18.

ACT ON IT Pass God's kind of care on to someone else today.

DIG ON Find out more about God's care for you in Psalm 91.

Talk About It • 4

EMPATHIZE: What's going on in your life?
ENCOURAGE: How are you doing with Jesus?
EQUIP: What one truth will you take home today?

- What do you expect to happen when you pray? (Study 16)
- When have *you* prayed—not gotten what you wanted—and felt grossly disappointed? Why don't you get an answer to every prayer? (Study 16)
- How would you explain God's answers to prayer to a friend who's hurting because God didn't give what he or she wanted? (Study 16)
- Why do you suppose God makes rules? (Study 17)
- What do you think is the right-here-right-now payoff for obeying God—putting his words into practice? (Study 17)
- Are you glad God spells out right and wrong for your life—or not? How come? (Study 17)
- Do you think God is a crusty old guy in the sky—and that his rules for living are too obnoxiously dated to bother following? Explain. (Study 18)
- True or false: God understood your world when he laid down a Bible full of do's and don'ts. (Study 18)
- Do you think God's commands still fit your world today? (Study 18)
- Do you ever worry that God wants to hunt you down and punish you? (Study 19)
- What has God promised to do with your sin? How does that make you feel? (Study 19)
- Tell how you'd explain it to a non-Christian: Why would anyone want to be a Christian? (Study 20)
- Do you think it's fair that God does great stuff for his followers—but plans punishment for anyone who rejects him? Explain your answer. (Study 20)

PART 5

UNTANGLING HEAVEN AND HELL

(21.) Who'da Thunk?
What happens when people die?

When the *Ultrastomachturner 3000* roller coaster locks up halfway around the eighth loop, you experience a few horrifying seconds hanging upside down with gallons of blood *whoosh*ing to your head—but only until the bolts holding your harness break. Then you flop out of your seat for a few seconds of free flight as you plunge two hundred fifty-six feet to the ground. "Who'da thunk," you mumble to yourself as you fall, "that my life would end like this?"

BRAIN DRAIN Okay: Take ten seconds and ponder the absolute inescapability of your own death. Now answer this: Precisely how scared do you get?

FLASHBACK Being nervous about death is normal—after all, it's the biggest moment of your life. Humans die, you might remember, because we all joined in Adam and Eve's first sin (Romans 5:12). And the Bible says a few more things about death. Like that you only die once, then face judgment (Hebrews 9:27) before God's throne (Revelation 20:11–15), where believers flock into Paradise and unbelievers rocket to punishment (Matthew 25:31–46). That's the big picture, but this Bible Chunk gets down to the nitty-gritty. You'll spot Jesus immediately after his friend Lazarus has died—and you'll get a picture of what God has in store for you.

BIBLE CHUNK Read John 11:11–27

(11) After he [Jesus] had said this, he went on to tell them, "Our friend Lazarus has fallen asleep; but I am going there to wake him up."

(12) His disciples replied, "Lord, if he sleeps, he will get better." (13) Jesus had been speaking of his death, but his disciples thought he meant natural sleep.

(14) So then he told them plainly, "Lazarus is dead, (15) and for your sake I am glad I was not there, so that you may believe. But let us go to him."

(16) Then Thomas (called Didymus) said to the rest of the disciples, "Let us also go, that we may die with him."

(17) On his arrival, Jesus found that Lazarus had already been in the tomb for four days. (18) Bethany was less than two miles from Jerusalem, (19) and many Jews had come to Martha and Mary to comfort them in the loss of their brother. (20) When Martha heard that Jesus was coming, she went out to meet him, but Mary stayed at home.

(21) "Lord," Martha said to Jesus, "if you had been here, my brother would not have died. (22) But I know that even now God will give you whatever you ask."

(23) Jesus said to her, "Your brother will rise again."

(24) Martha answered, "I know he will rise again in the resurrection at the last day."

(25) Jesus said to her, "I am the resurrection and the life. He who believes in me will live, even though he dies; (26) and whoever lives and believes in me will never die. Do you believe this?"

(27) "Yes, Lord," she told him, "I believe that you are the Christ, the Son of God, who was to come into the world."

STUFF TO KNOW At the start of this Bible Chunk, what do the disciples think Jesus is saying about Lazarus? Are they dense—or what (verses 11–13)?

What's actually happened to Lazarus (verse 14)?

SIDELIGHT Got that? Lazarus is good and dead. A few

verses after this Bible Chunk, you find out exactly how dead. " 'But, Lord,' said Martha, the sister of the dead man, 'by this time there is a bad odor, for he has been there four days' " (John 11:39).

Jesus knows Lazarus is dead, yet he says he's going to "wake him up." What does Jesus have planned (verses 11, 14–15)?

"Let us also go," Thomas says, "that we may die with him." What's up with that (verse 16)?

INSIGHT It's obvious this is a group of people who know a dead body when they see or smell one. The disciples know not only that Lazarus has died but that Jesus' life is in danger (John 5:18).

What does Jesus promise Martha (verse 23)? What exactly does he mean (verses 24–26)?

INSIGHT Jesus is going to solve Lazarus's immediate predicament. But he also makes a bigger promise—that everyone who believes in him will enjoy a resurrection that lasts forever.

BIG QUESTIONS If all of what Jesus says is true, should you be sad when someone dies (besides missing having them around)?

SIDELIGHT Strange thing: When Jesus found out Lazarus was dead, he wept—even though he already knew he was going to raise Lazarus back to life (John 11:35). Even this temporary death causes sadness too deep to stuff inside.

So what happens to Christians when they die?

SIDELIGHT Going to the grave isn't the end of the story for you: "I want you to know what will happen to the Christians who have died," Paul wrote, "so you will not be full of sorrow like people who have no hope. For since we believe that Jesus died and was raised to life again, we also believe that when Jesus comes, God will bring back with Jesus all the Christians who have died" (1 Thessalonians 4:13–14 NLT).

DEEP THOT In case you're wondering, Jesus did raise Lazarus from the dead. And he promises that those who believe in him *already* possess eternal life: "I tell you the truth, whoever hears my word and believes him who sent me has eternal life and will not be condemned; he has crossed over from death to life" (John 5:24). It's like he told Martha: Even if you die, you live.

STICKY STUFF God has some great plans for you: John 11:25–26.

ACT ON IT Mull this over: How does knowing that you have a home in heaven change how you think about death?

DIG ON Read more about your own post-death life in 1 Thessalonians 4:15–18.

22. To Valhalla or Not to Valhalla
What is heaven like?

Had you been a good Viking warrior dude in the days of old, you would have longed to die and head to Valhalla, the hall of slain heroes. In Valhalla, hearty men battle by day and banquet by night with Odin, king of the gods. Warriors are served by the Valkyries, a band of warrior-maidens. If you aren't chosen for Valhalla, however, you wind up in a dim underground world run by a goddess named Hel—daughter of Loki, the spirit of evil.

BRAIN DRAIN If you're a Christian, you've got a room booked in heaven for eternity. So what do you expect the place to be like?

FLASHBACK Heaven is more than a hope. It's a promise for people who believe in Jesus (John 14:1–3). Whether it feels like it or not, it's your real home (Philippians 3:20). Since you've got accommodations booked there for the rest of eternity, you might be wondering what it will be like—and who will be there. One hint: It ain't the Norse god Odin.

BIBLE CHUNK Read Revelation 21:1–8

(1) Then I saw a new heaven and a new earth, for the first heaven and the first earth had passed away, and there was no longer any sea. (2) I saw

the Holy City, the new Jerusalem, coming down out of heaven from God, prepared as a bride beautifully dressed for her husband. (3) And I heard a loud voice from the throne saying, "Now the dwelling of God is with men, and he will live with them. They will be his people, and God himself will be with them and be their God. (4) He will wipe every tear from their eyes. There will be no more death or mourning or crying or pain, for the old order of things has passed away."

(5) He who was seated on the throne said, "I am making everything new!" Then he said, "Write this down, for these words are trustworthy and true."

(6) He said to me: "It is done. I am the Alpha and the Omega, the Beginning and the End. To him who is thirsty I will give to drink without cost from the spring of the water of life. (7) He who overcomes will inherit all this, and I will be his God and he will be my son. (8) But the cowardly, the unbelieving, the vile, the murderers, the sexually immoral, those who practice magic arts, the idolaters and all liars—their place will be in the fiery lake of burning sulfur. This is the second death."

STUFF TO KNOW The start of this Bible Chunk
looks a bit like a movie scene—with an alien spacecraft a-hovering. So what's that thingie dropping out of the sky (verse 1)?

What happened to all the old stuff (verse 1)?

DA'SCOOP If you're at all attached to this planet, you
might read that verse and feel like Mom cleaned house and tossed out your Barbies or baseball cards. But *new* here doesn't mean that God trashed the old—but that he *remade* it. The *no sea* part also doesn't mean God is down on surfing. It means God has gotten rid of chaos.

What's the "Holy City"? What does it look like (verse 2)?

DA'SCOOP That *Holy City* is a place. But the *bride* part indicates it's also a bunch of people—God's people, to be exact, as perfect as a decked-out bride. Sounds confusing, but the image captures two concepts.

That's just what it looks like. What's the bigger deal about who is going to live there (verse 3)?

SIDELIGHT That theme screams through Scripture. God is preparing a people to live with him for eternity in heaven. Check out these *God-is-building-a-people* verses: Genesis 17:7; Exodus 6:7; Leviticus 26:12; Jeremiah 31:33; Ezekiel 11:20; 2 Corinthians 6:16; Hebrews 8:10; 1 Peter 2:9–10.

Where did pain and all those other ugly things go (verse 4)?

INSIGHT This is the perfection God planned for planet earth in the first place. It's the "very good" stuff you read about back in Genesis.

Who gets invited to this celestial resort (verse 6–7)?

INSIGHT God issues an open invitation to all: Revelation 22:17 says, "Whoever is thirsty, let him come; and whoever wishes, let him take the free gift of the water of life."

Who gets locked out? Where are they (verse 8)?

BIG QUESTIONS What happened to the streets of gold—and the harps?

SIDELIGHT That comes later in Revelation 21:9–27—along with emeralds, amethyst, and pearls. The harps are in Revelation 5:8 and 15:2, but it doesn't look like everyone gets one.

So if heaven is full of all that cool stuff, what do you suppose you'll stare at when you get there?

DEEP THOT Getting to see the stuff of heaven—whatever those awestriking images mean—is like going to a Hollywood party and looking no further than the appetizers. God is the real star of this party. The big deal about heaven isn't the *where* or even the *what*. It's the *Who*. And you'll be hanging with God and his friends forever.

STICKY STUFF Revelation 21:3–4 is a lot more fun than Valhalla.

ACT ON IT Talk to God about why you think heaven sounds like a great place.

DIG ON Take a peek at the rest of Revelation 21.

(23.) Sulfur Boils
Is hell real?

On July 8, 1741, New England pastor Jonathan Edwards preached his infamous sermon "Sinners in the Hands of an Angry God." Edwards rattled off cheery things like this: "The God that holds you over the pit of hell, much as one holds a spider, or some loathsome insect over the fire, abhors you, and is dreadfully provoked; his wrath toward you burns like fire; he looks upon you as worthy of nothing else, but to be cast into the fire." Sort of vivid, huh?

BRAIN DRAIN Do you think the idea of hell wrecks God's reputation with people? How come?

FLASHBACK You know that God is the righteous judge of the universe. But lots of people think Edwards makes him sound way too eager to toss sinners on the barby. Here are the Bible facts: *Hellacious Fact #1: Hell is real.* The Bible calls hell an "unquenchable fire" (Matthew 3:12), "damnation" (Matthew 23:33), a "fiery furnace" (Matthew 13:42, 50), "blackest darkness" (Jude 13), and a "fiery lake of burning sulfur" (Revelation 21:8). *Hellacious Fact #2: Hell isn't where God wants you to be.* But how can a good God cook up such a sizzling place?

BIBLE CHUNK Read Revelation 20:7–15

(7) When the thousand years are over, Satan will be released from his prison (8) and will go out to deceive the nations in the four corners of the

earth—Gog and Magog—to gather them for battle. In number they are like the sand on the seashore. (9) They marched across the breadth of the earth and surrounded the camp of God's people, the city he loves. But fire came down from heaven and devoured them. (10) And the devil, who deceived them, was thrown into the lake of burning sulfur, where the beast and the false prophet had been thrown. They will be tormented day and night for ever and ever.

(11) Then I saw a great white throne and him who was seated on it. Earth and sky fled from his presence, and there was no place for them. (12) And I saw the dead, great and small, standing before the throne, and books were opened. Another book was opened, which is the book of life. The dead were judged according to what they had done as recorded in the books. (13) The sea gave up the dead that were in it, and death and Hades gave up the dead that were in them, and each person was judged according to what he had done. (14) Then death and Hades were thrown into the lake of fire. The lake of fire is the second death. (15) If anyone's name was not found written in the book of life, he was thrown into the lake of fire.

STUFF TO KNOW Bible buffs disagree about how and when this first bit of good vs. evil action plays out—but who is Satan trying to deceive (verse 8)?

And who is Satan trying to snuff out (verse 9)?

So how does God punish the devil for his deceit—not just this once, but throughout history (verse 10)?

INSIGHT The Beast and the False Prophet you might recognize from the book of Revelation were tossed into the burning sulfur back in Revelation 19:20.

Most folks don't dislike the idea of Satan—the one the Bible shows as the head of all things evil—getting toasted. But who faces God's judgment next (verses 11–12)?

INSIGHT "Earth and sky fled from his presence" is a poetic way of saying that at this moment of judgment for all humankind, everything besides God fades to insignificance.

A couple of books are opened. What for (verses 12–13)? Who gets spared from the lake of fire (verse 15)?

INSIGHT That Book of Life is a concrete way of saying "the people who belong to God" (Revelation 13:8, 17:8, 21:27). Some Bible buffs, by the way, argue that this scene only includes people whose names are *not* written in the Book of Life, since Christians "have already passed from death into life" (John 5:24 NLT).

BIG QUESTIONS Do you think hell is a good idea? Explain.

INSIGHT Hell sounds harsh, but we wouldn't have it any other way. Hell shows the evilness of evil. It displays the rightness of God. It fulfills justice. It helps us know evil really does get punished. And oddly enough, hell confirms our freedom. That's freaky. But it's true.

Why do people wind up in hell?

INSIGHT Whatever flames and boiling sulfur picture about hell, what really makes the place *hell* is being totally banished from God's good presence. Hell gives its occupants an eternity of what they've chosen in this life: an existence without God. And like Billy Graham has said, "God will never send anybody to hell. If man goes to hell, he goes by his own free choice. Hell was created for the devil and his angels, not for man. God never meant that man should go there." The huge medieval Italian poet Dante Alighieri (1265–1321) wrote that "If you insist on having your own way, you will get it. Hell is the enjoyment of your own way forever."

How can people escape hell?

DEEP THOT Hell is a choice, because God offers people a way out of judgment. Romans 6:23 says, "For the wages of sin is death, but the gift of God is eternal life in Christ Jesus our Lord." You can tell God you know that Christ died in your place. You can thank him for providing forgiveness for you. And once you start your new life with God, being close to him lasts forever.

STICKY STUFF Revelation 20:15 is a hearty reminder to hang on to God.

ACT ON IT If you want to know more about heaven—and hell—grab a copy of my book *Look Who's Toast Now!*

DIG ON See what Jesus has to say about hell in Matthew 10:28.

24. TEOTWAWKI
Is Jesus coming back?

"Let me get this right," says your best non-Christian friend. "You think that one day Jesus is coming back to earth? On the clouds? No visible means of support? And that when he shows up it will usher in the-end-of-the-world-as-we-know-it?" To each question you nod your head *yes*. "Well," says your friend, "that's even weirder than thinking Jesus rose from the dead."

BRAIN DRAIN How weird is it to believe Jesus is coming back to earth? Explain.

FLASHBACK Eyewitnesses say that Jesus was last seen on planet earth, ascending into the clouds. And the Bible claims he's coming back in the same style he exited (Acts 1:10–11). At the tail end of this Bible Chunk Jesus made totally clear the fact that only his Father knows when he will return (Matthew 24:36) and that his "second coming" will surprise even his followers (Matthew 24:25–41). That's no excuse to stop thinking about his arrival. Instead, he says, "keep watch, because you do not know on what day your Lord will come"(Matthew 24:42).

BIBLE CHUNK Read Matthew 24:21–31

(21) For then there will be great distress, unequaled from the beginning of the world until now—and never to be equaled again. (22) If those days had not been cut short, no one would survive, but for the sake of the elect those days will be shortened. (23) At that time if anyone says to you, 'Look,

here is the Christ!' or, 'There he is!' do not believe it. (24) For false Christs and false prophets will appear and perform great signs and miracles to deceive even the elect—if that were possible. (25) See, I have told you ahead of time.

(26) "So if anyone tells you, 'There he is, out in the desert,' do not go out; or, 'Here he is, in the inner rooms,' do not believe it. (27) For as the lightning that comes from the east and flashes to the west, so will be the coming of the Son of Man. (28) Wherever there is a carcass, there the vultures will gather.

(29) "Immediately after the distress of those days

" 'the sun will be darkened,
and the moon will not give its light;
the stars will fall from the sky,
and the heavenly bodies will be shaken.'

(30) "At that time the sign of the Son of Man will appear in the sky, and all the nations of the earth will mourn. They will see the Son of Man coming on the clouds of the sky, with power and great glory. (31) And he will send his angels with a loud trumpet call, and they will gather his elect from the four winds, from one end of the heavens to the other."

STUFF TO KNOW "For then," Jesus says, "there will be great distress." Exactly *when* is he talking about (verse 21)?

INSIGHT Not so fast. A tiny fraction of Bible buffs believe Jesus is predicting events around the fall of Jerusalem in A.D. 70 But Jesus seems to be talking about a one-of-a-kind, world-ending event. Unless you think Jesus is totally yanking your brain, it's safe to conclude he is talking about the future.

How bad is that "great distress" going to get? How do you know (verses 21–22)?

What kind of fakes can you expect to be wandering around (verses 23–25)?

INSIGHT Jesus is saying that before his return you'll spot people not just pretending to be saviors for the world (verse 24) but lots of people who believe them (verse 23).

So does Jesus think you'll confuse his coming with the claims of these crazies? How come (verses 26–27)?

There's more. What will the big splash of his coming look like (verses 29–30)? Who all will see this go down (verse 30)?

Hmmm . . . that sounds hard to miss. What else will happen when Jesus arrives from heaven (verse 31)?

INSIGHT That's the event Bible buffs call "the rapture." Though you can find some serious disagreements about *how* and *when* the rapture happens, this Bible Chunk leads you to an inescapable conclusion that Jesus *is* serious about coming back—and he's coming back for his people.

BIG QUESTIONS So how would you explain any of this to a non-Christian friend?

INSIGHT Bible prophecy fascinates lots of non-Christians. But for those who call you crazy, start instead with the historical and biblical evidences for the Resurrection—and let them see how your expectation of Christ's return makes a difference in your life. More on that in DEEP THOT. . . .

Do you think Christ's return is scary—or stupendous?

What good does it do you to know any of this stuff?

DEEP THOT Near the back end of the Bible, Peter wrote, "But the day of the Lord will come like a thief. The heavens will disappear with a roar; the elements will be destroyed by fire, and the earth and everything in it will be laid bare. Since everything will be destroyed in this way, what kind of people ought you to be? You ought to live holy and godly lives as you look forward to the day of God and speed its coming" (2 Peter 3:10–12). So look forward. And live holy.

STICKY STUFF You've got Jesus' promise in Matthew 24:30.

ACT ON IT Decide today on one way you're going to change your life because Christ's coming again is true.

DIG ON Check Matthew 25 to learn how to keep watch.

25. Rest Assured
Is my faith just made up?

It's not a dream. You're sitting on a beach, post–high school, chatting with a non-Christian friend. And here's what you might say if you keep thinking hard about the mind-boggling questions of your faith: "I had a lot of doubts slamming around in my brain," you explain. "My whole faith seemed kind of iffy to me. But first I figured out it was okay to ask questions—and then I started to find answers. You know, no two people have the exact same doubts and questions. But I've found out that God has honest answers to all of them."

BRAIN DRAIN So are you convinced of the truth of your Christian faith? What did it for you—or what do you still need?

FLASHBACK Back at the beginning of the Bible book of John, Jesus applauds Nathanael for asking tough questions (John 1:47). In this Bible Chunk, Jesus talks to the disciple most folks know as "doubting Thomas," coaching him to belief. This Bible Chunk recognizes that it's normal to need convincing about spiritual truth. It points out that the Bible was written so that you can believe—and not just to have factoids crammed in your head but to find a radically good life close to Jesus.

BIBLE CHUNK Read John 20:24–31

(24) Now Thomas (called Didymus), one of the Twelve, was not with the disciples when Jesus came. (25) So the other disciples told him, "We have seen the Lord!"

But he said to them, "Unless I see the nail marks in his hands and put my finger where the nails were, and put my hand into his side, I will not believe it."

(26) A week later his disciples were in the house again, and Thomas was with them. Though the doors were locked, Jesus came and stood among them and said, "Peace be with you!" (27) Then he said to Thomas, "Put your finger here; see my hands. Reach out your hand and put it into my side. Stop doubting and believe."

(28) Thomas said to him, "My Lord and my God!"

(29) Then Jesus told him, "Because you have seen me, you have believed; blessed are those who have not seen and yet have believed."

(30) Jesus did many other miraculous signs in the presence of his disciples, which are not recorded in this book. (31) But these are written that you may believe that Jesus is the Christ, the Son of God, and that by believing you may have life in his name.

STUFF TO KNOW It's eleven against one: What do the other disciples want Thomas to believe (verse 25)?

What will it take to prove that to Thomas (verse 25)?

INSIGHT The phrase "told him" means the disciples repeated—and repeated—their claim that Jesus was alive. Thomas wanted nothing less than hard evidence of the Crucifixion—and the Resurrection. That's a good thing: His doubts disprove the argument that Jesus' resurrection was a mass hallucination or wishful thinking. Thomas was there. He asked the tough questions you might ask. And he got answers.

What happens a little later? How does Jesus get in (verse 26)?

SIDELIGHT Just as Jesus had appeared to his disciples in John 20:19, he enters through a locked door. Yet the disciples weren't greeting a ghost. They could touch his hands and side. And in John 21:13, Jesus ate. His resurrected body was the same but somehow different—like the funky body the Bible promises you in heaven (2 Corinthians 5:1–4).

Jesus invites Thomas to poke at the wounds inflicted on the cross. How come (verse 27)?

Thomas doesn't do it, but what does he say instead (verse 28)?

INSIGHT Jesus doesn't bash Thomas. He offers him the evidence he wants, repeating words he wasn't around to hear. By now Thomas has seen enough to be convinced. Both titles Thomas uses for Jesus—Lord and God—were names you'd only use for God himself.

What was the whole reason John wrote his Bible book about Jesus (verse 31)?

BIG QUESTIONS You didn't get a chance to touch Christ's side or feel the nail wounds in his hands. How can you believe in him without having seen him?

INSIGHT By this point you've figured out that God wants you to found your faith on more than gooshy feelings. The Bible accurately presents God's history with humankind. It's where you get the facts about Jesus. While you don't get to see him, you can still believe—on the basis of the evidence—that "Jesus is the Christ, the Son of God." And by believing, you will have "life in his name."

God doesn't intend for you to merely stuff your head full of spiritual factoids. How are you letting the facts of your faith change your life?

DEEP THOT The great Christian teacher Oswald Chambers (1874–1917) said that getting smart about your faith is a life-altering experience: "Jesus Christ was not a man who twenty centuries ago lived on this earth for thirty-three years and was crucified," he wrote. "He was God Incarnate, manifested at one point of history. . . . The presentation of this fact produces what no other fact in the whole of history could produce: the miracle of God at work in human souls." So get smart. Get close to Jesus. And let your knowledge of him change your life.

STICKY STUFF Remind yourself why the Bible was written with John 20:31.

ACT ON IT What mature Christian do you have in your life who will let you ask hard spiritual questions?

DIG ON Grab a glance at the last chapter of John—John 21—for yet another amazing appearance by Jesus.

Talk About It • 5

EMPATHIZE: What's going on in your life?
ENCOURAGE: How are you doing with Jesus?
EQUIP: What one truth will you take home today?

- How scared are you about dying? (Study 21)
- What happens to Christians when they die? (Study 21)
- If you're a Christian, you've got a room booked in heaven for eternity. So what do you expect the place to be like? (Study 22)
- What's the biggest thing you look forward to about heaven? (Study 22)
- Do you think the idea of hell wrecks God's reputation with people? How come? (Study 23)
- Do you think hell is a good idea? Explain. (Study 23)
- How is hell a choice? How can people escape hell? (Study 23)
- Is it strange to believe that Jesus is coming again? Do you think Christ's return is scary—or stupendous? (Study 24)
- What will the big splash of Jesus' return look like? Can you mistake it for anything else? (Study 24)
- So are you convinced of the truth of your Christian faith? What did studying this book do for you—or what do you still need? (Study 25)
- God doesn't intend for you to merely stuff your head full of spiritual factoids. How are you letting the facts of your faith change your life? (Study 25)

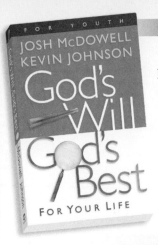

Understanding God's Will for Your Life

Happiness, a good career, good friends, and closeness with God are desires of everyone's heart. This book explains that God also desires to give these things to you—He even provides a specific plan for you to experience each of them. There's no catch, but there is a condition, a condition you can't afford to miss!

God's Will, God's Best
by Josh McDowell and Kevin Johnson

Because faith isn't just for sundays

Real As Life

Sick of stories featuring characters you can't relate to? The new BRIO GIRLS novels introduce you to a group of teens as true to life as your own friends. Jacie, Becca, Hannah, and the rest live lives as complicated and fun as your own, and you won't believe some of the choices they face in dealing with boys, family, school, friends, and more. A must-read series for fiction fans, these are stories written just for you!

BRIO GIRLS created by Lissa Halls Johnson
Stuck in the Sky
Fast Forward to Normal
Opportunity Knocks Twice
Double Exposure

Source Code: BOBGW

BETHANYHOUSE

11400 Hampshire Ave S. Minneapolis, MN 55438
(866) 241-6733 www.bethanyhouse.com